Notes &
Queries

VOLUME 6

Notes & Queries

VOLUME 6

edited by

Joseph Harker

FOURTH ESTATE • *London*

First published in Great Britain in 1995 by
Fourth Estate Limited
6 Salem Road
London, W2 4BU
Copyright © 1995 by Guardian Newspapers Ltd

The right of Joseph Harker to be identified as the compiler of
this work has been asserted by him in accordance with the
Copyright, Designs and Patents Act 1988.

A catalogue record for this book is available from the British Library.

ISBN 1–85702–373–0

Typeset by Palimpsest Book Production Limited,
Polmont, Stirlingshire
Printed in Great Britain by Cox & Wyman Ltd, Reading, Berks

QUESTION: I am baffled by reading of sporting contests 'going to the wire'. Is there a link with escaping prisoners of war?

☐ IT COMES from horse racing in the 19th-century United States. The start and finish lines were marked by a wire suspended across the track – high up, of course. So a close race was uncertain 'right down to the wire'.
John Ridge, Clitheroe, Lancs.

☐ THE phrase has its origins in US sports journalism. Before the days of long distance telephone, reporters covering the evening's baseball games would often have to leave the event early to telegraph their report back to the editor's desk. 'Going to the wire' told readers that a game's outcome was still in doubt when the reporter was wiring his report.
Nick Clay, Nottingham.

QUESTION: Why, when we used to have them, were ticket collectors on buses called 'conductors'?

☐ WHEN I was a bus conductor in the 1960s, we were responsible for issuing tickets to passengers; but the rule book I carried listed the conductor's duties as checking that the destination and service number were clearly displayed; checking that the bus departed on time; calling out the names of the main stops on the route; controlling the stopping and starting of the bus by use of the correct bell signals; assisting passengers entering and leaving the bus; ensuring the number of standing passengers did not exceed the legal maximum,

etc. The most interesting responsibility was keeping a lookout, on moorland routes, for intending passengers who might be sheltering from adverse weather conditions. In short, a conductor managed most of the affairs related to the running of the bus.
Michael Thompson, Cheadle, Cheshire.

QUESTION: By what criteria can the extent to which a country is civilised be assessed? Which are the most civilised countries?

□ THIS can be easily determined by whether or not the state practises capital punishment. The degree of civilisation can be measured by the elapsed time since the last execution and by the percentage of the public that is against the return of the death penalty. Thus the UK is now moderately civilised, but precariously so.
Toby Moore, Canberra.

□ 'CIVILISATION' derives from the Latin *civis* and *cognates*, meaning citizen and relating to concepts of city-dwelling. So, the criterion by which civilisation could be measured is the extent to which a country's population lives in cities. Thus, Britain would be more civilised than, say, France; and the United States and Japan would probably be amongst the most civilised countries. Of course, in practice, civilisation is really a loaded assessment of moral and cultural superiority, which also derives from European perceptions of Classical antiquity and the early Mediterranean city states. It is therefore useless as an objective framework for thinking about societies. A recent trend has been to associate 'civilised' with 'humanitarian', but this is no more helpful, since only wealthy nation states can usually afford to be humanitarian to their neighbours.
J. Dronfield, Cambridge.

□ IN THE words of Mahatma Gandhi: 'A nation's status of civilisation can be measured by the way it treats its animals.'
Ute Cohen, Las Vegas, Nevada.

□ PROBABLY the best answer was provided by the late Norbert Elias in 1939 (*The Civilising Process*, Blackwell, Oxford, 1995). Elias shows how 'civilisation' was originally a French term which connoted a process. Gradually, however, it came to express the self-image of the dominant classes and countries in the West, acquiring in that connection the meaning of a state of affairs which had already been achieved. It also came to imply, as a corollary, antithetical pair-terms such as 'barbarism' which were used to denigrate non-western countries and peoples, weaker western countries and, for a long time, the lower classes in the West itself. Elias also shows how, in the course of their rise to world power, people in countries such as Britain and France underwent 'civilising processes' as measured by such criteria as: the formation of relatively stable and internally pacified states; growing wealth; moves in the direction of the democratisation of political institutions; the establishment, starting with the upper classes, of forms of manners and etiquette through which greater regard for others is expressed; and the emergence of forms of conscience in terms of which overt violence is abhorred. Elias regarded these processes as reversible and did not believe they had gone very far. He speculated that people in a more civilised future, should it be achieved, will probably regard even the most advanced peoples of today as 'late barbarians'. In *Studien über die Deutschen* (1989), Elias showed how the dominant trend in the development of Germany did not follow this generally 'civilising' path. Germany did not become a unified nation state until 1871 and did so under the leadership of the militaristic Prussians. This meant that forms of authoritarian rule became entrenched, leading to opposition to democracy as 'un-German', a brutalisation of large sections of the middle classes through a cult of duelling in the universities, and eventually to a breakdown of civilisation in the Weimar years. It was in this context that the extremely 'de-civilising' rise of Hitler and the Nazis and the Holocaust occurred.

Eric Dunning, Professor of Sociology, University of Leicester.

QUESTION: Since the bank is entitled to charge me anything up to £15 for the administration costs involved in having to write to me, am I entitled to charge them if I have to write because they have made a mistake on my account?

☐ I ASKED my bank to transfer £1,175 from one account to another, but it transferred £117,500 – leaving one account £115,000 overdrawn. It then started charging me interest on my 'unarranged overdraft'. It took me three letters and numerous phone calls to sort out the error. I charged the bank £100 and it eventually, and reluctantly, paid.

Barry Thomas, Ashbourne, Derby.

☐ I HAVE successfully charged my bank for the cost of phone calls, car parking, my own time in writing a letter to them and, most recently, £30 for some misinformation and a series of mistakes that took several letters and phone calls to sort out. If everyone did this then the service might eventually improve.

Martin Dutnell, Crawley, W. Sussex.

QUESTION: Has anyone on *The Antiques Road-show* ever obtained the market value quoted by the experts for their exhibits?

☐ THERE have been numerous occasions over the 17-year span of the programme when the price estimates have been achieved and exceeded in subsequent sale. The most recent example was a painting of cats by Henrietta Ronner, bought at a car boot sale for 50p, estimated on the Inverness Roadshow at £15,000 and subsequently sold at Christie's for £22,500. Successes of past series include a lost painting by the Victorian artist Richard Dadd estimated at £100,000 and subsequently bought by the British Museum for slightly more.
Christopher Lewis, executive producer, The Antiques Roadshow.

QUESTION: What could we do if it became obvious that either the Queen or the Prime Minister had gone completely mad?

☐ THERE are precedents for both situations. Monarch: tolerate the situation until the public demand action, then appoint a Prince Regent. Prime Minister: tolerate the situation for two general elections, then appoint John Major.
Colin Taylor, Aughton, Ormskirk.

☐ THE questioner implies a 'terminal' event, but the reality would be less dramatic. If the Queen or Prime Minister developed a mental illness they would be able to seek treatment in the normal way. If they lacked the insight to do this, they could become the subject of a Mental Health Act Assessment. If this resulted in temporary detention in hospital, there is an obligation in the case of the Prime Minister (or any MP) for the speaker of the House to be informed. No special provisions exist for the royal family. The political consequences of such an event occurring in the case of the Prime Minister can only be surmised; but clearly they are related to the duration, severity and likely prognosis of the condition as well as to the current political situation. In the case of the Queen, apart from other members of the royal family taking on some of her duties during any period of illness, I doubt whether there would be any cause to remove her: although were the illness a chronic one she might be persuaded to abdicate.

D. S. Allen (consultant psychiatrist), High Wycombe, Bucks.

□ HARDER to answer is what do you do with an electorate which appears to have gone the same way?
Roger Davis, Pontypridd, Mid Glamorgan.

□ IN ANSWER to Roger Davis, Parliament should follow Brecht's advice: dissolve the electorate and elect a new one.
A. Rudolf, London N12.

QUESTION: In a recent article on the Froncysyllte aqueduct, the *Guardian* quoted Telford as stipulating no more than three narrow-boats to be on it at one time. Why? Surely the number of boats does not make any difference to the weight on the piers?

□ THE questioner is correct. A barge floats due to the Principle of Archimedes. That is to say, the volume of water displaced by the vessel weighs the same as the barge and its contents. Consequently, everything is in equilibrium. Incidentally, when the aqueduct was opened

on 26 November 1805, six boats crossed the structure in a procession. The engineers were in the fourth one, suggesting they had a fair degree of confidence in their aqueduct.
Philip Parker, Senior Project Engineer, British Waterways, Northwich, Cheshire.

☐ I EXPECT they had in mind the weight of the draught-horses on the towpath!
T. Bolton, Orrell, Lancs.

☐ THE questioner should stop thinking about pier pressure. If the aqueduct contains more than three boats, there will not be enough water left in the trough to allow them to progress efficiently. Taken to an extreme, if the aqueduct had narrow boats nose to tail along its length, there would be an almost total displacement of water.
R. A. Stewart, Hanwell, London W7.

☐ R. A. STEWART is surely wrong when he says that 'if the aqueduct had narrow boats nose to tail along its length there would be an almost total displacement of water'. The displacement of water would indeed be equal to the combined weight of the boats, but it would be spread along the total length of the canal, making no significant change to the depth of water on the aqueduct.
Harry Rushton, Cheshire.

☐ BOATS *would* increase the weight on the piers if the aqueduct were sealed tight by lock gates at each end, and the boats lowered into the water from a crane; then all the displaced water would stay in the channel and the weight on the piers would increase. This doesn't happen normally when a boat enters the aqueduct as the displaced water flows out into the canal at either end. If we could compute the total pressure exerted on the bed of the whole

length of the canal, we would find that any extra boat in
the water adds to the pressure briefly until the displaced
water flows out of the nearest overflow – or indefinitely if
the water level is lower than the maximum. The aqueduct,
being a part of that canal bed, must take a share of that extra
pressure, however small and insignificant in practice.
David Nelson, Dunfermline, Fife.

**QUESTION: What is the origin of the expression 'blue
murder'?**

☐ THE phrase is used where an American would say
'bloody murder', and perhaps 'blue' is simply a last-minute
substitute for what was once considered an offensive adjective. *Morbleu!* (Zounds!) is an archaic French expletive
ultimately from *'mort Dieu!'* that may have turned up in
English as 'blue murder' by folk etymology.
Jim Ransom, Palo Alto, California.

**QUESTION: I have read that at sunset in the tropics,
as the sun passes beneath the horizon, a 'green flash' is
seen. Is this a real phenomenon, and when and where
might it be seen?**

☐ THE green flash is caused by the earth's atmosphere
bending the sun's rays so that, towards sunset, the apparent
position of the sun is some two degrees higher than its
real position. Short wavelength light at the blue/green
end of the spectrum is bent more than *long* wavelength
light at the red end. This means that there are separate
overlapping images of the sun with blue/green at the top
and red at the bottom. When the sun sets, the blue/green
fringe is the last to sink below the horizon and, no longer
swamped by light from the main disc of the sun, is briefly

visible. Observations of the green flash are not confined to the tropics and can, on occasion, be seen almost anywhere with a clear horizon when atmospheric conditions are right. If the disc of the setting sun appears very reddened, the green flash is unlikely to be seen because most of the short wavelength blue/green light has been scattered out by atmospheric particles.

Philip G. Griffiths, consultant ophthalmologist, Newcastle General Hospital.

☐ THE flash has a number of slightly variant forms – it may be a thin band just above the sun's disc and it may be blue or violet or even changing. It can even occur before the sun starts to set and there may be a 'red flash' below the sun. The green flash was first popularised by an 1882 novel of Jules Verne, *Le Rayon vert*, about a search for it. Though described by Lord Kelvin in a letter to *Nature* in 1899, it was long generally believed to be some sort of visual illusion. Attempts to photograph it with an ordinary camera are futile as the flash is too small to register on the film. It was not until 1954 that colour photographs were obtained using specially adapted telescopes at the Vatican Observatory at Castel Gandolfo.

David Singmaster, London SW4.

☐ THE 'green flash' is much sought on the north coast of Cornwall. I have seen it twice – once from Newquay and, more recently, returning from an evening walk to Stepper Point, near Padstow.

Keith Richards, London N12.

QUESTION: Is artistic creativity largely the preserve of those with liberal or left-wing sympathies?

☐ YES. Artistic creativity is rarely motivated by financial

gain and is therefore not of interest to those on the right.
Paul Harvey Howlett, Surbiton, Surrey.

☐ MANY artists of undoubted accomplishment are, if not
self-professed right-wingers, certainly critically evaluated
as such. If we take the field of literature, the list includes
modern poets T. S. Eliot, Ezra Pound and W. B. Yeats;
the novelists John Braine, Ayn Rand, Henry Williamson;
playwrights such as Terence Rattigan. The list can be
extended to include Ernst Jünger and Louis Ferdinand
Céline, not to mention the proto-fascist movement of the
Italian Futurists. Furthermore, all artists suffer greatly
from personal defects and there are just as many cruel
and selfish left-wing artists as there are right-wing ones.
Robert Murray, Wanstead, London E11.

☐ AS A psychologist, I made a study of two types,
traditional and radical. The Trads have values which
embrace the family, justice, law and order, persistence
and solid achievement. The Rads on the other hand are
artistic, creative, inventive, impulsive and innovative. The
Rads are more likely to see faults in a situation and to
devise means of putting them right. This trait creates
problems. No sooner have Rads formed a group which
is devoted to changing a situation than off-shoots arise
within the group which see better ways of doing the
job. Hence Trads tend to join one simple 'conservative'
party, whereas the Rads spread out into several central or
left-wing liberal groupings. I would expect more artistic
creativity among the left.
Dr Geoffrey Watson, Winchester, Hants.

☐ POLITICAL sympathies of any persuasion are arrived at
via a series of judgments and rationalisations. Creativity,
however, is a timeless quality without measure and is not
a slave to the arrogance of the human thought process.

Therefore creativity and political sympathies are mutually exclusive.
Christine Nunn, Bletchingley, Surrey.

QUESTION: How do people who hate mints or are allergic to them cope with oral hygiene products?

☐ AS SOMEONE who hates the taste of mint, I have found that if we want to grin, we have to bear it.
D. O'Neill, Bollington, Cheshire.

☐ BECAUSE of allergy I use herbal toothpaste – which can be bought at any good chemist or health food shop – and a herbal mouthwash from my herbalist.
I. A. Tolley, Okehampton, Devon.

☐ I USE Eucryl tooth powder (formulated for smokers) in its original flavour. A suitable mouthwash is original Corsodyl, whose flavour is reminiscent of liquorice. There is also a chocolate-flavoured toothpaste available for children, but I cannot face sampling it.
Margot Agnew, Chorley.

☐ FIFTY years ago my uncle, a farmer in Lancashire, used salt to brush his teeth, and salt water to sniff up his nose to clean his nasal passages. Chimney soot was said to be effective for cleaning teeth. I tried it once: my teeth were dazzling white, but only in contrast to my black gums.
Shirley Ward, Ardross, Western Australia.

☐ THERE are many oral hygiene products which are not mint-flavoured, such as Mentadent P original toothpaste or original Plax mouthwash. For children there is no major problem as many children's toothpastes are fruit-flavoured.
Pauline Blaney, Heriot-Watt University, Edinburgh.

QUESTION: Bob Dylan recorded a song called 'Hurricane' about an American boxer, Ruben Carter, who was allegedly victim of a miscarriage of justice. Did the song obtain his release from prison?

☐ THE American middleweight boxer Ruben 'Hurricane' Carter was given a life sentence in 1966 for the murder of a bartender and two of the bar's customers. Carter maintained that he had been framed. His story is set out in his biography, *The Sixteenth Round*. Bob Dylan wrote 'Hurricane' in 1975 with the help of Jacques Levy. There are clear allegations of racism and incompetence in the legal proceedings. For instance, Dylan has 'the cops' telling one witness: 'We want to pin this triple murder on him, he ain't no Gentleman Jim.' Carter's campaign for a retrial was helped by the support of Dylan and other celebrities. But after having enjoyed a taste of freedom pending this new trial, Carter was again found guilty and reimprisoned. He was given two consecutive and one concurrent life sentences. The triple murder convictions were finally overturned in November 1985. After 19 years in prison, Carter was again released on bail. Subsequent attempts to restore the convictions were rejected by the US Supreme Court.

G. A. Wilkinson, Waterlooville, Hants.

QUESTION: *The Oxford English Dictionary* spells 'realise' as 'realize' without any 's' alternative. When did this spelling change occur, and why?

☐ THE spelling 'realise' is first recorded in *The Oxford English Dictionary* in a quotation from W. Taylor dated 1689, and the first example of 'realize' is 1611. However, lexicographers seem to have regarded the former either as non-standard, or as too regular a variant to be worth listing, and it did not appear as an explicit alternative in *The Concise Oxford Dictionary* until 1964. This may have been prompted partly by the fact that, by then, contemporary editions of other publishers' dictionaries were boldly erring the other way by failing to mention the '-ize' form. Subsequent editions of the smaller Oxford dictionaries have included both variants, but the full-size dictionary does not always list regular variants such as '-ise' forms for every single word. The two spellings of this suffix have always co-existed in British use, but there has been a trend over the last century towards spellings in '-ise'. This is due partly, perhaps, to the influence of French; partly to over-correction on the false analogy of 'comprise', 'televise', etc. (which have an etymological root in -is-); and most of all to the mistaken but widespread belief that '-ize' spellings are Americanisms.

Jeremy Marshall, Oxford English Dictionaries, Oxford.

☐ GREEK had *zeta* (z). Latin didn't. When Greek '-izô' words were taken into Latin, 'z' became 's'. So English words are spelt '-ize' in the Greek, or '-ise' in the Latin, way. The 'z' versus 's' difference is one way in which the Oxford and Cambridge University presses express their differentness, and deny the validity of each other's spelling. Oxford favours Greek; Cambridge Latin. The rest of us can suit ourselves.

Alison Adcock, Oxford.

QUESTION: Can plants develop cancer?

☐ ABNORMAL growths are common in plants but they are rarely the creeping malignant types associated with animal cancers. Common forms are the various cankers (same etymology) usually manifested as abnormal bark growth on trees. These are caused by parasitic attack, usually fungal. The bizarre growth distortions known as plant galls are perhaps the most familiar examples of plant cancers. These are caused by parasitic agents ranging from viruses to insects and parasitic plants. The gall is an abnormal growth of host tissue stimulated by the parasite infection and is usually structured to provide some service (usually shelter and/or food) for the parasite.

Jonathan Briggs, Nailsworth, Glos.

☐ TOBACCO is well known for the cancers it helps to develop.

Simon Walsh, Braintree, Essex.

QUESTION: Seventh Heaven. What are the other six?

☐ IN THE Cabbala, a Jewish mystical system of technology and metaphysics was developed, mainly between the 9th and 13th centuries. It was maintained that there are seven heavens, each rising in happiness above the other. In this cosmology the lower heaven was the region of the stars; the highest, also known as the heaven of heavens, was the abode of God and the most exalted angels. This classification passed into Islamic theology in which the first heaven is of silver and in it are the stars, each with an angel warder and strung out like lamps on golden chains. This is the abode of Adam and Eve. The second heaven is of gold and the domain of Jesus and John the Baptist. The third is of pearl and allotted to Joseph; here Azrael writes the names of new-borns in a large book from which he expunges the names of the newly dead. The fourth heaven, of white gold, is Enoch's. Here dwells the Angel of Tears, who ceaselessly sheds tears for the sins of man.

The fifth heaven is Aaron's and is of silver. The sixth heaven, which is of ruby and garnet, is presided over by Moses; here dwells the Guardian Angel of heaven and earth, half snow and half fire.
Geoffrey Taunton, Portsmouth, Hants.

□ GEOFFREY TAUNTON'S answer was informative, but the Cabbalistic version of the cosmos he describes was itself co-opted from an ancient Greek concept. Their six concentrically nested heavenly spheres were supposed to be composed of an essential, crystalline substance, and to each was fixed one of the known heavenly bodies: Sun, Mercury, Venus, Mars, Jupiter and Saturn. The moon occurred in the corrupted earthly realm, as evidenced by its visible blotches (the maria), and so was not accorded its own sphere. Seventh heaven, which became associated with the Judaeo-Christian Empyrean, occurred above the ultimate sphere encompassing and directing all the rest – the Primum Mobile.
Jim Costa, Museum of Comparative Zoology, Cambridge, Mass.

QUESTION: Does the ostrich's defence of burying its head in the sand work?

□ THE ostrich that buries its head is a myth, like the lemming that charges into the sea. As Bergan Evans says in his book *The Natural History of Nonsense*: 'The most vital of all the mythical birds is the ostrich that buries its head in the sand at the approach of danger . . . It is too precious to die . . . what would politicians, preachers and prophets do without the conventional metaphor of this ornithological fiction?'
David Cottis, London SW15.

QUESTION: Do growers find any commercial value from the fruit of the tea bush or the leaves of the coffee plant?

☐ ACCORDING to Purseglove's *Tropical Crops*, the dried leaves of the coffee bush are used as an infusion in Indonesia and Malaysia, while a close relative of the tea plant, *Camellia sasanqua*, is reportedly grown in China and Japan for the oil extracted from the seeds. However, growing a shrub for its leaves requires drastic measures: continual plucking, and radical pruning every four years in the case of tea. It never gets the chance to flower, let alone set seed, unless it reaches a height of 3 metres. Conversely, the coffee bush needs long and droopy lateral branches for a decent crop of beans. The leaves on these branches are probably no good for drying and infusing. Is there any crop which can produce valuable leaves and fruit together?
Roland Lubett, NSW, Australia.

☐ IN THE 1950s George Haggar, a Lebanese coffee grower in the South Sudan, put dried coffee leaves on sale as a substitute for tea. He called them *shaibun*, a combination of the Arabic for tea (*shai*) and coffee (*bun*). They were not a great success.
J. K. Jackson, Pinner, Middlx.

QUESTION: What is the origin of the phrase 'taking the biscuit'?

☐ THE origin lies in the strict protocol observed in the early to middle ages in the royal court, especially in matters concerning food. With so much fear over the prospect of poisoning, particularly by badly stored meat,

it was customary for the head of the table to be offered first choice rather than having food served directly on to his/her plate. It became an honour for a special guest to 'take the best cut'. In time this became corrupted to 'taking the biscuit'.
John Wald, Belfast.

☐ LIKE its American equivalent, 'taking the cake', the phrase is originally from ancient Athens, where a small cake or biscuit was a traditional prize in athletic and artistic contests. The expression is used in Aristophanes' play *The Poet and the Woman* (411 BC).
David Cottis, London SW15.

QUESTION: How was the 50th anniversary of the Battle of Waterloo commemorated in 1865?

☐ IT WAS not publicly celebrated in Britain at all, though Wellington used to mark the anniversary each year with a private banquet until his death in 1852. *The Times* of 4 July 1865 reports, with distaste, that the anniversary was celebrated in the Netherlands 'with an enthusiasm which approximated to patriotism run mad'. A triumphal procession of allegorical chariots was staged, 'accompanied by a distinguished assemblage of the great unwashed'. The celebration was said to be 'highly disapproved of by a large majority of the middle and upper classes of Dutch society' and the King pointedly left the capital and went hunting in order to make clear his objections to 'the patriotic follies of his subjects'.
Jill Allbrooke, British Newspaper Library, London NW9.

☐ WELLINGTON'S army included a German contingent of 6,000 Brunswick troops. In June 1865 some 900 of these

reassembled in the town of Brunswick in north-western Germany. The veterans participated in parades, a cathedral service, a banquet and a display of fireworks and military music. An eyewitness account of these festivities appears in *The Eagle's Last Triumph: Napoleon's Victory at Ligny* (Greenhill Books, 1994). Waterloo's 180th anniversary was celebrated in June 1995 with a large re-enactment on the battlefield. The night before there was a sound and light spectacular at the Lion Mound.
Andrew Uffindell, International Napoleonic Society, Berkhamsted, Herts.

QUESTION: How can I tell the difference between good art and bad art?

☐ IF YOU can afford it, it's bad.
Annie Leymarie, London NW3.

☐ FORGET perspective and composition. Ignore line, form and colour. Discount the pundits and the critics. If, when you look at a painting or a sculpture, a tingle goes down your spine, it's good art for you.
Ann Garwell, Pontypool, Gwent.

☐ IT'S the same as telling the difference between good and bad people, wine, music, etc. It takes attention, caring and intimacy. Don't spurn what doesn't immediately appeal to you; and don't just go around awarding or withholding marks. Art (like those other things) isn't there merely to be judged.
Norbert Lynton, Brighton.

☐ ONLY by waiting! Good art is that which continues to be thought to be good. Composers such as Schmidt and Spohr were at the time thought to be the equal

of their contemporary Beethoven. But only Beethoven's reputation survives the test of time.
Michael Meadowcroft, Leeds.

☐ JOHN RUSKIN'S *Modern Painters* (Everyman edition) states: 'I do not say that the art is greatest which gives most pleasure, because perhaps there is some art whose end is to teach, and not to please. I do not say that the art is greatest which teaches us most, because perhaps there is some art whose end is to please, and not to teach. I do not say that the art is greatest which imitates best, because perhaps there is some art whose end is to create, and not to imitate. But I say that the art is greatest, which conveys to the mind of the spectator, by any means whatsoever, the greatest number of the greatest ideas . . .'
Albert Adler, London N4.

QUESTION: Did John Logie Baird (or his descendants) profit from his invention of television?

☐ IN HIS notes for an autobiography, published in *Sermons, Soap and Television* (Royal Television Society, 1988), Baird states that his company, Television Limited, went into receivership, and his share of what was left amounted to £3,000. At one time his paper holding in the company was worth a quarter of a million pounds. He made and spent a lot of money during the days of TV Ltd; and the Baird Television Company, of which he was to become president, paid him £4,000 in 1937. Shortly after the declaration of war in 1939, the company called in the receiver and Baird's contract was terminated.
Tom Singleton, Shere, Surrey.

☐ UNFORTUNATELY John Logie Baird did not 'invent' television and probably nobody outside Britain has even heard of him. The fundamental part of any television system is the scanner – the device that breaks the picture into elements which can be converted into electric impulses. Baird used a scanner invented by the German Paul Nipkow over 40 years earlier, and linked it to photo-electric cells. But his system was incapable of anything more than poor-quality picture definition and was prone to mechanical breakdown. Despite this, towards the end of the 1920s the BBC was persuaded to adopt the Baird system for experimental transmissions. There was little or no chance of long-term success with it, but it believed there was some kudos in being the first to televise anything at all. Meanwhile, others had been working on a completely different system of electronic scanning using an adapted cathode ray tube. The Russian-born American Vladimar Zworikin was a leading inventor in this field, and this system eventually became the basis of today's television.

Don Benlow, Wisbech, Cambs.

☐ DURING the 1930s my father received a good salary as a director of the Baird Television Co. We had a large house at Sydenham, near the company laboratories at Crystal Palace. But as your correspondent Tom Singleton states, Baird never made a fortune from shares or royalties. After he died in 1946 my mother received a modest pension from the Baird Company. That was about it as far as 'profits' were concerned. Controversy rages on about whether mechanically scanned TV was 'the real thing'. It was certainly the only viable form of television from 1925 until about 1935. Your correspondent Don Benlow errs in saying that Baird's name is unknown outside Britain. The Americans recognise Baird as the first with television, and I have given lectures to interested audiences in the US and Canada. The first television transmission across the Atlantic, in 1928, was reported with banner headlines in

the *New York Times* and it was a great spur to television research in the US. As far as other countries are concerned, a friend has sent me a long article about Baird in China's television magazine. Australia's major television awards, the Logies, are named after my father.
Malcolm Baird, Department of Chemical Engineering, McMaster University, Ontario.

□ How sad that no one mentioned Alan Dower Blumlein who, having sorted out all the fundamentals of stereo sound in the 1930s, headed the team at EMI which produced the first television pictures using electronic scanning. He was a true engineer and inventor, and audio and video systems still make use of the basic elements of his work.
Chris Woolf, Liskeard, Cornwall.

QUESTION: Why does corn pop? Is there a natural benefit?

□ THERE are five different types of corn: sweet, dent, flint, pod and popcorn. Popcorn, the only type that pops, has a kernel containing carbohydrate (principally starch), protein, fat and water. Water is stored in a small circle of soft starch. As the kernel is heated, the water turns to steam, building up pressure. When the harder surface surrounding the starch finally gives way, the soft starch is forced out and the corn pops.
Barry Gower, Director, Pop Corn Crazy, Pinner, Middlx.

QUESTION: How is visibility determined by an automatic weather station, as on shipping forecasts?

□ THE definition of 'visibility' varies; in daylight it is defined as the greatest distance at which it is just

possible to see and identify a prominent dark object
against the horizon sky. At night the same criteria apply
for an unfocused, moderately intense (about 25 candelas)
light source. Scattering of light is the phenomenon which
accounts for most loss of visibility experienced at the
earth's surface. Measuring the scatter coefficient thus gives
a direct relationship to the visibility. An automatic weather
station (AWS) can use a visibility meter, which measures
the scatter coefficient of the light emitted from a xenon
flash lamp forward-scattered by the atmospheric particles.
The output of the visibility meter can be expressed
as a measurement of visibility in terms of distance,
i.e. kilometres or nautical miles. It can measure quite
accurately from 50 metres to 50 km.
*Peter J. Godwin, AWS Manager, Met Office, Bracknell,
Berks.*

**QUESTION: What is the term for the fear of talking
to a telephone answering machine?**

☐ TELEMERITY?
Mike Collins, Loughborough, Leics.

☐ A HANG-UP.
Geoff Black, Cambridge.

**QUESTION: If in 1946, following the almost complete
exhaustion of the economy after the second world war,
we could afford the Welfare State – including universal
education system and the free National Health Service
– why can these necessities not be afforded now?**

☐ AFTER the second world war, Britain was as de-
institutionalised as it has ever been. Almost all the power

and wealth were in the hands of government. An electorate which had learnt many things during the war about the way our country had been run – by the few, for the few – returned to power a party committed to change. But it did not change the established structure. The institutions recouped their lost ground over the post-war decades, and the few, who had lain low over these decades, found their opportunity, through a single-minded ideologue, to roll back the post-war achievements. Tony Blair claims to want to change back again; but without changing the underlying structure, power and wealth will always flow from the poor to the rich.
Bill Mason, Beckenham, Kent.

QUESTION: Assuming that most Saxon, Norman and medieval communities would have required a varied mix of skilled people in order to survive, why are there so many Smiths in relation to Weavers, Coopers, Bakers and Wrights? And What did Jones do originally?

☐ SMITHS were very good at picking chastity belts.
Brendan Cooper, Hammersmith, London.

☐ HAVING worked all day on something hot and sweaty, it obviously came naturally to continue at night. I realise that this does not explain the relative lack of Rogers but I shall leave this to others more expert than I.
Maurice Childs, Bromley, Kent.

☐ THE prevalence of smiths presumably dates from the many centuries when the only mode of transport was a horse. So every town – however insignificant – would have had its own smithy. Perhaps not everyone had a cart (or the wheel rims didn't wear out so fast); so there were not so many wrights, nor much call for barrel-makers (coopers), bakers or weavers. As for Jones, this is a shortened form for Johnson – and similar abbreviation applies to Evans, Williams, Hughes, Davis, etc.

Graham R. Jones, Withington, Manchester.

☐ IT IS wrong to conclude that there were more smiths than wrights or coopers. Small variations in the frequency of names, which happen by chance, are magnified as the generations pass. I made a computer simulation of a village of 100 couples, with 20 each of Wrights, Smiths, Jones, Coopers and Weavers. I assumed that every couple makes 10 attempts to reproduce, and that each attempt has a 1 in 10 chance of success. This ensures that the population stays roughly stable. The simulation ran for 50 generations (about 1,000 years). I tried it 200 times, and the results varied greatly. Usually one or more names die off altogether, and it is very common for one or two names to become dominant. If we could wind back to AD 1100 and start again, the dominant name might turn out to be Weaver or any of the others.

Chris Brew, Edinburgh.

☐ SMITH is from the same root as Smitan, which means 'to smite', and is one of the few Old English bynames to be recorded a century before the Norman Conquest. Smith of the 10th century was a worker in iron, smiting ingots into swords, shields, battle-axes, halberds and ploughshares. But the occupational term 'smith' embraced other workers who smote their raw materials; it lost its precision and new names were needed. They were found in another Old English word *wryhta* 'wright or craftsman', subsequently dividing into Cartwright, Wheelwright, and Wainwright (maker of wains or waggons). With increasing special-isation, a distinction had to be made between a worker in iron and a worker in tin, so more exact definitions were made, hence blacksmith and whitesmith. The smith was an

important man in medieval times, making and repairing swords, lances, defensive ironworks for castles and manor houses, offensive engines for assaulting enemy castles, and peaceful items such as agricultural implements. He was the technologist and technician, the engineer and mechanic of his day. There are several reasons why Smith is such a widespread surname; it is one of the oldest Anglo-Saxon names, so Smiths have been around longer than most. The Smiths of Old England were a strong, lusty, vigorous people capable of raising large families. Smiths were much in demand in medieval and later times; every village had its smithy with one or more smiths working profitably in it, so they and their families are unlikely to have gone hungry in English winters when food was scarce. Because he was not quite so close to the heat of battle in medieval warfare as Archers, Bowman (Bowmen), Knights, and others, Smith probably returned safely to his native village after the war, to resume his work and the care of his family.
Kenneth Allen, Cook, Australia.

QUESTION: If I put bigger wheels on my car – say 30 per cent bigger – I will travel 30 per cent further for every turn of the wheels. Does this mean I can travel 30 per cent further on a tank of petrol?

□ No. IN order to propel the vehicle, the engine must produce a turning force at the wheel hub, so that by Newton's first law the corresponding reaction at the rim (i.e. the point where the tyre touches the ground) directs the vehicle forwards. The force required at the hub varies with the distance between the hub and the point of exertion (known as 'the moment'), and thus an increase of 30 per cent in radius will require a corresponding increase in the turning force to produce the equivalent forward motion. The engine would have to work harder, with an increase

in fuel consumption, so no net gain would result. The frictional forces of small wheels are generally greater than those of larger ones, due to bearing design, so there could be a small increase in efficiency with suitable gearing. If this were not true, car design would have evolved to the point where wheels the size of castors would be widespread, increasing the amount of usable space inside the vehicle to the detriment of the aesthetics!
Adrian Lea, North Shields, Tyne and Wear.

☐ I TRIED bigger wheels on my Mini. The only obvious advantage was that it stopped dogs peeing in through the window.
Jeff Williams, Ystrad Mynach, Mid Glamorgan.

QUESTION: From where does the word 'quid' originate?

☐ THE Irish word *cuid*, meaning 'share', is commonly used in phrases such as *'cuid mhaith airgid'* – a good deal of money. It is possible that the word transferred to English slang use via Irish-speaking soldiers in the British Army.
Tony Scanlan, Clarinbridge, Co. Galway, Ireland.

☐ *THE Oxford Dictionary of Etymology* gives the origin as 18th-century slang for a sovereign or guinea, derived from the Latin *quiddam*, meaning 'something'. An alternative derivation might be from the French *quibus*, 'the wherewithal'.
Michael Hutton, London SE5.

☐ IT IS a contraction of the Latin phrase *quid pro quo* which has come to mean a reciprocal agreement. Bank notes carry the wording 'Promise to pay the bearer . . .' which constitutes such an agreement. Therefore, when £1

notes were the most common variety, they became known as 'a quid'.
Robin Webb, Winchester, Hants.

QUESTION: How does one become a wine taster or perfume developer? Is there a course that gives you a recognised certification?

☐ THE University of Plymouth has now become the centre for a world-wide correspondence course in perfumery. We are dispatching 'homework kits' to students as far afield as Russia, Australia and India. The kits contain 100 vials of perfume and aromatic materials, together with manuals dealing with such things as odour identification vocabulary, essential oils, aromatic chemicals and derivatives of essential oils. Students receive a full briefing on the art and application of perfumery. Then they work through these manuals – undertaking a series of odour identification sessions using samples from the kit – and submit odour and academic exercises to the tutors for assessment. The project, leading to a diploma in perfumery, is validated by the International Federation of Essential Oils and Aroma Trades.
Ken Seymour, University of Plymouth.

QUESTION: I heard that the rule in French where the past participle 'agrees' with the verb was artificially introduced to make the language more complex and therefore more 'noble'. Is this true?

☐ THE French past participle doesn't agree with the verb, but with the subject or, sometimes, the object. It wasn't artificially introduced; it just follows logic. The past participle agrees with the subject when it is used with

the auxiliary '*être*' ('to be') because it acts as an adjective, which must always agree in French.
Anne Harry, Hereford.

QUESTION: How far and how fast would I have to walk, cycle or swim for it to be the equivalent of running a marathon?

☐ IF ONE stood and watched the London marathon, the casual fun-jogger would have a heart rate (HR) of about 70 beats per minute; a reasonable runner about 60; and a top athlete about 50. The fun-jogger takes, say, 5 hours to complete the race averaging a HR of 130; the runner takes 3 hours at an average HR of 160; and the athlete takes 2 hours 10 minutes at an average of 190. So the extra number of heartbeats to run a marathon rather than watch it is about 18,000 for all three. But the athlete pumps more blood per heartstroke (about 0.175 litres compared to 0.125 litres for the workrate of a normal person). Also, many people have an abnormal heart rate for some time after a marathon before their body gets back to equilibrium. For a reasonably fit person with a standing-about HR of 60, the equivalent exercise would be walking from Wasdale campsite to the summit of Scafell (90 minutes, average HR 140); spending the next 3 hours fossicking over Scafell Pike, Great End and the Gable Traverse; then descending to Wasdale (average HR 120). Total distance, 9 miles.
Mike Hayes, Sheffield.

☐ THE average man uses 100 calories (440 kilojoules) when running a mile, so will use 2,600 calories in a marathon. The answer would vary between individuals, but walking has about the same energy cost per mile as running; cycling uses up about 45 calories per mile; and swimming, being much slower, uses up between 300 and 400 calories per

mile. Roughly, a swimming marathon equivalent is 7 miles; cycling 60 miles; and walking 26 miles. 'How fast?' is a meaningless question, since all finishers, no matter how slow, have 'run a marathon'.
Bruce Tulloh, Marlborough, Wilts.

☐ NO CYCLIST would accept Bruce Tulloh's conclusion that a marathon is equal to 60 miles on a bike. My father, on his 80th birthday, cycled 80 miles, but there's no way he could have run 100 yards. I have always regarded the 12-hour time trial, in which a reasonably good club cyclist might expect to cover 250 miles, as the natural equivalent to the marathon. And I don't think that Mike Hayes's conclusion, in which he describes a good day's walk in the Lake District, makes sense either. There are many reasonably fit fell-walkers for whom a marathon would be unthinkable. Perhaps something like the Lyke Wake Walk (about 40 miles across the North York Moors) might be somewhere nearer to a marathon equivalent.
Roger Wilkinson, Belper, Derby.

QUESTION: Has anyone information about *Billy's Weekly Liar* from the 1950s?

☐ PRINTED on the *Liar* itself: 'Published by Bolton's Publishers (Regd) at Walton-le-Dale, Preston.' They were single newsprint sheets 15″ x 10″, with jokes and stories printed on both sides, five for a shilling by mail order.
A. A. Waddicor, Fernhill, Bristol.

☐ MY RECOLLECTIONS of the publication date back about 80 years. It was about A4 size, and was produced from premises known as Billy's Shop. I doubt if it appeared weekly. It was full of wisecracks, such as the advice to someone who had lost something: 'Go to Helen Hunt for

it.' The shop sold tricks and jokes, and there was also some electrical equipment. Promotion was carried out by Billy's Band which consisted of two somewhat decrepit performers who paraded the streets of Preston. As they walked along in the gutter, the leader beat a big drum and the second man blew on a trumpet.
S. Seed, Lancaster.

☐ *BILLY LIAR* has now become the government's unemployment and inflation statistics.
R. J. Golden, Hull, N. Humberside.

☐ IT WAS regularly sold inside and outside Preston North End football ground during the 1950s and 1960s and I last purchased a copy when it was selling for threepence. Although 'Billy's' is long demised, its spirit lives on in the excellent *Preston Pie Muncher* fanzine. When informed of an unlikely fact, many older Prestonians still reply: 'Has tha bin readin' *Billy's Weekly Liar?*'
Ken Robinson, Preston.

QUESTION: Why do weather forecasters never mention the Irish Republic?

☐ WE REALISE that many people in the Republic can receive both ITV and BBC transmissions, and I am assured that our presenters do mention the Republic on some of their forecasts – especially when weather crossing or affecting the Republic will be moving towards the UK. But the presenters often have to stand in front of the section of weather charts featuring the Republic, thereby obscuring the symbols that are routinely positioned over the country!
Andy Yeatman, Met Office, Bracknell, Berks.

☐ ANDY YEATMAN said presenters have to stand in front of the Republic, thereby obscuring the symbols. So what will the Met Office do when the country is reunited? Are the presenters to be replaced by taller people or will they just be given a box to stand on?
Roger Tennent, Ullesthorpe, Leics.

QUESTION: When and for what were tickets first issued?

☐ THE first tickets were issued in 1454. They were Indulgences granted by Pope Nicholas V to those who gave money to help the campaign against the Turks, who had taken Constantinople the previous year. Indulgences were slips of paper granting remission of the punishment due to sin after absolution. Most from that period were handwritten but those issued in Mainz were printed (predating the Gutenberg Bible), with blank spaces for the donor's name. Effectively, they were tickets to Heaven.
John Farrow, Department of Library and Information Studies, Manchester Metropolitan University.

☐ ALL civilised urban communities would have needed tickets of some kind. In ancient Athens, tickets were needed for admission to the theatre, the lawcourts, the Assembly, and other places attended by large gatherings of people. There was a small fee for attendance as a juryman at the lawcourts, or as a voting citizen at the Assembly: this could be obtained on production of one's ticket. The tickets were usually stamped discs of metal or terracotta: a great many have been found, and are described and illustrated in Sir Arthur Pickard-Cambridge's book *The Dramatic Festivals of Athens*. The earliest surviving specimens date from the end of the 5th century BC.
David Barrett, Oxford.

QUESTION: What is the highest ever recorded IQ? Does it mean anything?

☐ IN THE late 1980s *The Guinness Book of Records* cited an IQ score of 228 achieved by the aptly named Marilyn vos Savant. IQs used to be calculated by dividing 'mental age', as measured on a standardised test, by actual age and then multiplying by 100. But nowadays it is defined statistically as a normal distribution in which scores are assigned so that 50 per cent of the population score above 100 (the population average), 16 per cent score above 115, 2 per cent score above 130, and so on. This means that about one person in 100 million billion can be expected to score 228 or above. Given the world's population of about 5 billion, the odds against anyone having such a high IQ are more than 20 million to one. This suggests that either Ms vos Savant's IQ is meaningless, or she is a walking miracle. If she is a miracle, she must have the intelligence to realise that her IQ is meaningless. Even if it were credible, it would not be the highest IQ ever recorded. In *Pygmalion Reconsidered* (1971), Elashoff and Snow reveal that Rosenthal and Jacobson, researching the effects of teacher expectations, recorded IQs of 249, 251, 262 and 300 in a single San Francisco primary school. The meaningfulness of IQ scores is debatable but experts agree that no IQ test can be trusted to measure accurately outside the range 60 to 160.
Dr Andrew M. Colman, Department of Psychology, University of Leicester.

QUESTION: If a Gents is closed, is there anything in law stopping me from nipping into the Ladies?

☐ SOME years ago, at a baseball stadium in Baltimore, a young woman in the long queue snaking out of the

Ladies noticed that the Gents seemed empty. She nipped in – and was arrested, amid much media attention, for disturbing the peace. She went to court, sued the stadium for discrimination (since the number using the Ladies far outweighed those using the Gents) and won.
Jill Walden, Baltimore, Maryland.

☐ THERE will be a queue in the Ladies – don't bother!
Rachel Mear, Leicester.

QUESTION: All brewers use 'finings' to clarify beer. Finings are a form of isinglass, made from the swim bladders of an oriental sturgeon, dissolved in acid. How or why did anyone ever think that this slimy substance would be beneficial to making beer?

☐ ISINGLASS is, I believe, still widely used for beer but has gone out of fashion for wine. Gelatine and bentonite are widely used for bulk wines. The properties required of finings are that they should coagulate particulate matter and then itself separate out, adding as little as possible to the liquid itself. Given the gluey mess left after cooking a fish, it is unsurprising that a fish byproduct should be discovered to have suitable properties. One reason for the move away from isinglass, apart from the price, is that it takes a lot out of the drink, leaving a less tasty brew.
Ivan Viehoff, Chesham, Bucks.

☐ IF ISINGLASS and gelatine are used in wine and beer production, does that render them unacceptable to vegetarian diets?
Rona Dunbar, Edinburgh.

☐ VEGETARIANS should scrutinise labels for ingredients of foods and beverages, but unfortunately they will normally

find no mention of processing aids, such as animal-derived fining agents used to clarify and chill-proof wines, beers, ciders and fruit-juices. Brewers and vintners are still not required even to declare the ingredients and additives in the alcoholic drinks. However, increasing resort is being made to mineral earths and other non-animal filtering aids; or the drinks are kept for some time to allow sediments to settle out. But cask-conditioning usually entails use of finings objectionable to vegetarians.
Alan Long, VEGA, Greenford, Middlx.

☐ IT IS not necessary to use animal (or fish) products in the clarification of wine although some winemakers certainly do. Bentonite clay (produced in Cornwall) is an excellent alternative. It is almost certain, however, that no trace of finings could be found in wine following filtration. My own winemaking policy is never to use animal products for clarification.
Rob Lindo, Camel Valley Wine, Bodmin, Cornwall.

QUESTION: If I light one candle in a dark room, then place a mirror beside it, to reflect it, is there an actual increase in the amount of light in the room?

☐ No. THE light from the candle is either absorbed or reflected by any surface on which it falls. The result of placing the mirror is that the wall behind it receives less light than it would if the mirror were not there. The wall in front of the mirror receives a little extra. Some, but not much, of the light will be absorbed by the mirror itself. The absorption of light causes a small rise in the temperature of the surface. Because the energy of the light would be very small, the temperature rise would be small also.
Dudley Turner, Westerham, Kent.

□ DUDLEY TURNER is wrong. While there is no more light being generated in the room, there *is* more light passing through the room. Light which would have been absorbed by the wall is reflected back across the room by the mirror, so at any point in the room you have the light coming directly from the candle plus the extra light which first went away and was then reflected back by the mirror. The effect is the same as having another candle slightly less bright than the first. The maximum illumination in the room is achieved by covering all the walls with mirrors so that only a tiny amount is absorbed at each reflection and the rest is bounced backwards and forwards through the room. The effect of this hall of mirrors would be the same as being surrounded by hundreds of candles of diminishing brightness placed at increasing distances from the first.
G. M. Berriman, Wakefield, W. Yorks.

QUESTION: What is the origin of circles with arrows and crosses as male and female symbols?

□ THESE symbols are among those that have been used since ancient times to represent the various gods and goddesses. The circle with an arrow means Mars and the circle with a cross underneath means Venus. Later, doctors and naturalists began to use them as a shorthand for male and female, apparently in the questionable belief that Mars, the god of war, and Venus, the goddess of love, typified the sexes. The Mars symbol denotes a circular shield resting on a spear; while Venus's vanity about her appearance is represented by a hand-held looking-glass. If the latter interpretation is correct, the symbol's adoption by feminists is one of history's subtler ironies.
John Bryant, London N5.

☐ THERE IS more to the signs than offered by John Bryant. Originally the male sign was simply the inverse of Venus's mirror, with a cross over the orb. The cross represents the human situation, the intersection of the horizontal earth line with the vertical heaven line, indicating the equilibrium between our instincts and the rationality of society. The circle represents a further dose of nature, which the male surmounts and controls, while the female learns to carry.
Will Milne, London N4.

QUESTION: I recently married but have retained my own name. When I went to a solicitor to revise my will, he insisted this must be in my 'married name'. Was he right?

☐ THIS is nonsense. Names are essentially a useful convention whereby we can identify individuals. The law allows us to use such names as we see fit, provided that we are not trying to deceive. Most of us stick to one name but this is not necessary. The questioner can make a will in any name she chooses. If, when she is dead, she has always used her birth name then her death certificate will show that. The will will then match and cause no problems. If she has used a different name, the application for probate of her will should explain this fact.
Gerry Martin, School of Law, University of Northumbria.

QUESTION: Are the Bob Hoskins adverts for BT the most irritating TV ads ever?

☐ NO. THEY are beaten by any ads featuring Danny Baker.
Tom Barnard, Leicester.

□ CLEARLY the ads are highly effective, having stuck in
the questioner's mind. The 1970s Shake 'n' Vac ad may
not have been to everyone's taste but how many people
over 25 do not know that the product puts the freshness
back? It's good to irritate.
Phil Woodford, London NW3.

**QUESTION: What is the origin of the expression 'hair
of the dog', used when combating a hangover with
another drink?**

□ THIS expression, more fully quoted as 'applying the hair
of the dog that bit you', originates from the superstitious
belief that rabies could be averted by applying to the
bite a dressing made from the hair of the animal which
caused the injury. The parallel between this and the
cure for a hangover of taking a nip of the very stuff
which caused it is fairly obvious, and was known even
to Athenaeus:

> Take the hair, it is well-written,
> Of the dog by which you're bitten;
> Work off one wine by his brother,
> And one labour with another . . .

Ken Cumberlidge, London E11.

□ FURTHER to Ken Cumberlidge's answer, this same
principle had a very useful application during the 17th
century in the theory of the weapon-salve. This held that
a battle wound could best be healed by the application of
a salve extracted from the actual weapon that had caused
it. In 1631 this gave rise to a pamphlet duel between the
Hermetic philosopher Robert Fludd, who supported the
method, and a certain William Foster who opposed it

because he felt it worked through diabolical means.
Paul Cheshire, Bath, Avon.

QUESTION: Is there a difference between Holland and the Netherlands; if so, what is it?

☐ IT IS rather like the difference between England and Britain. The Netherlands is divided into 12 provinces, two of which are North Holland and South Holland, containing Amsterdam, Den Haag (the Hague) and Rotterdam. Properly, the other Dutch provinces – such as Utrecht or North Brabant – are not part of Holland, only part of the Netherlands. This confusion (between England and Britain, Holland and the Netherlands) is made by other Europeans, too: a French person will typically refer to anyone from Britain as '*anglais*', and to anyone from the Netherlands as '*hollandais*'.
Ian O'Neill, Whiteparish, Wilts.

☐ FURTHER to Ian O'Neill's reply: in the 16th and 17th centuries, when the Dutch were a great seafaring people, all the Netherlands' main ports were located in either north or south Holland. So sailors on their travels would explain that they came from Holland.
F. Kok, Lincoln.

QUESTION: How good a legal case would the Catholic Church have if it were to claim ownership of all the current Anglican buildings that existed before the Reformation?

☐ WITH the restoration of Charles II in 1660, the Church of England recovered possession of the buildings from which it had been excluded during the Commonwealth.

It had owned these buildings continuously since their foundation following the Christianisation of England. The setting up of the *Roman* Catholic hierarchy in England in the 19th century as a separate, schismatic body of dissenters from the Church conveys no legal, moral or theological claim to any buildings other than its own.
Revd John MacDonald Smith, Norton, Worcs.

☐ THE Revd John MacDonald Smith is quite wrong to state that the Church of England has owned the church buildings of this country since their foundation. First, the C of E only came into existence with the Elizabethan Settlement of 1569; and second, church buildings are (in English law) the property of the clergy not of the Church. Hence a parish church is the legal property of the parson, while a cathedral is the property of the cathedral chapter. This has created, at various times, the possibility of the clergy returning ancient churches to their former, Catholic use. Initially, this was because the clergy of 1569 consisted entirely of pre-Reformation priests with broadly Catholic sympathies. Subsequently, there was perceived to be a danger that Catholic lay patrons might appoint covert Catholics to Anglican livings; or that a Catholic monarch might appoint Catholics to crown livings and cathedral chapters. A series of penal laws – specifically aimed at Roman Catholics – have been passed to prevent this happening, and these are explicitly restated in the Roman Catholic Relief Act of 1829.
Tom Hennell, Withington, Manchester.

☐ IF THE law recognised spiritual influence or traditional values, the pagans and the Jews might combine to make an equally good bid for possession of the Vatican's assets.
A. Meltzer, London SE3.

☐ TOM HENNELL is quite wrong when he perpetuates

the old myth about the Church of England coming
into existence with the Elizabethan Settlement of 1569.
It remained the same church except that the authority of
the Bishop of Rome was no longer recognised within the
realm. The Church of England remained and still remains
the Catholic Church in this land, by law established.
A. Tomlinson, Congleton, Cheshire.

QUESTION: How do you cure a broken heart?

☐ DON'T panic – normally a broken heart is not fatal. At
the very least you will learn to cope with the pain. A broken
heart is the occupational hazard of loving someone. Learn
from the experience as much as you can. Try to see if there
is a pattern that corresponds with previous relationships.
Remember how it feels to be hurt in this way, and resolve
to avoid causing such pain to others. Mourn your lost love
– cry, weep, wail, gnash your teeth, tell your friends all
about it. And then get on with the rest of your life. At
least a broken heart can mend – some people have no
hearts at all!
G. Beasley, Leicester.

☐ CONCENTRATE on the least attractive features of the
beloved: physical imperfections, mannerisms, the way
he/she didn't get on with your best friends, anything.
Ideally you should convince yourself that you were never
even happy together; if not, it at least dulls some of the
worst of the pain.
John Nurick, New Malden, Surrey.

☐ How does a parish priest cope when his wife has died of
cancer? By visiting the bereaved and sharing their sorrow.
Prayer sometimes means just sitting in a room with a
bereaved person while they shed the tears of their grief

without saying anything. Often more can be conveyed by a silent handshake or a hug than through volumes of words. The totally unexpected pay-off is that our own burdens are lightened and one gains new insight into the meaning of the Crucifixion and of Easter morning. The Lord is Risen indeed and broken hearts are mended. Paradoxically, the cure for a broken heart is to share the sorrows of others. I believe this is because the faculty through which we experience great sorrow is one with the faculty through which we experience our greatest joys.
(Revd) Alfred Willetts, Chester.

QUESTION: Where does the expression 'the world is his oyster' come from?

☐ SHAKESPEARE (*The Merry Wives of Windsor*, II, ii) uses the phrase 'the world's mine oyster', meaning that the world is the place from which to extract profit, as one would extract a pearl from an oyster.
Kevin Luff, London SE13.

QUESTION: What exactly is wrong with wearing an anorak?

☐ NOTHING. It alerts the rest of us to the presence of a train-spotter, allowing us to take evasive action.
Dave Blackhurst, Bridgnorth, Shropshire.

☐ WAS this question by any chance e-mailed?
Ian Shuttleworth, London N8.

QUESTION: Under what circumstances is it illegal to park on the pavement?

☐ THE situation in Greater London is clear. Under section 15 of the GLC (General Powers) Act it is an offence to 'park a vehicle with one or more of its wheels resting on a footway (i.e. pavement), central reservation or grass verge on any road in Greater London, which is subject to a speed limit of 40 mph or less'. This law is still in force, but it is up to individual boroughs to enforce it. In the rest of the country the situation is less clear. Under the Highways Act (1980), it is an offence 'wilfully' to 'obstruct . . . free passage' along the pavement 'without lawful authority or excuse', but examples of obstruction given are: putting advertising boards on the pavement and displaying shopware on the pavement. Under the Highways Act (1835), it is an offence to 'drive' on the pavement. However, it seems that attempts to prosecute drivers for parking on the pavement under this law have failed because drivers were not seen to drive on the pavement. Under section 7 of the Road Traffic Act (1974) it is an offence to park on pavements, verges or central reservations. However, this section has not been enacted despite urgings from local authorities. By a law of 1812 sponsored by Lord Ellenborough: 'Every unauthorised obstruction of a highway to the annoyance of the King's subjects is an indictable offence . . . no one can make a stableyard of the King's highway.' In other words, anyone leaving their vehicle stationary on the pavement (or even at the kerbside) can be summoned for unreasonable use of the road, even if this is not causing an obstruction.

D. Kelly, Greater Manchester Pedestrians' Association, Sale, Cheshire.

QUESTION: In Brian Friel's play *Dancing at Lughnasa*, one of the characters (Maggie) poses a riddle which no one answers: 'Why is a gramophone like a parrot?' Can anyone solve it?

☐ THEY are both pollyphonic.
T. Jones, Gravesend, Kent.

☐ THE parrot, like the gramophone, reproduces His Master's Voice.
Charles Lewis, Surbiton, Surrey.

QUESTION: Why do chefs wear such silly hats?

☐ TO KEEP loose hair out of food when cooking, some head covering is necessary. A close-fitting cap such as those worn by meat porters would be unpleasantly sweaty in the hot, humid atmosphere of a kitchen. The chef's hat provides some ventilation.
M. H. McDougall, Kingston upon Thames, Surrey.

☐ THERE seems to be a law that makes headgears explode upwards. Chefs' hats 100 years ago were quite sensible caps. Top hats between 1800 and 1850 grew by a foot. The Bigoudennes' bonnets in Brittany grew between 1900 and 1950 by the same amount. The enormous crests of military helmets began as low ridges to deflect club or sword. Bishops mitres grew equally. Professional or national assertiveness probably underlies this gigantism.
Hans Schwarz, Greenwich, London SE10.

☐ THE main reason is ranking. Historically, master chefs wore a black pillar-box type hat so that they could be easily identified within a large brigade of chefs. Executive chefs now wear a large toque for the same reason. Pastry chefs wear a large floppy hat to denote the section that they are working in, also to stop their ears and necks burning when they carry hot pastry trays on their shoulders. More junior chefs wear skull caps. Some chefs believe that wearing a

large hat allows air to circulate, which stops them from going bald.
Dai Davies, Captain, Welsh Culinary Team, Llangollen, Clwyd.

☐ AFTER the fall of Constantinople to the Turks in 1452 and the subsequent occupation of Greece, many professional cooks chose to enter monasteries to cook for the brethren. They preferred the comparative safety of the religious house rather than being exposed to the sometimes capricious taxation of the local Turkish Beys. For these unordained members of the community the monkish black stove-pipe hat was changed to white and has since remained as the insignia of the professional chef.
Henry Mein, Bleasby, Notts.

QUESTION: Is it possible, anywhere in the world, to buy tinned parrot? If not, what other unusual items can be bought in cans?

☐ I THOUGHT that was what tinned Spam was.
G. Campbell, Newtownabbey, Northern Ireland.

☐ A FRIEND once showed me a tin of elephant chunks in gravy which had been sent to him by a friend in South Africa. However, since he was a vegetarian, the tin is still unopened.
David Harper, London E1.

☐ WHILE working at the Savoy Hotel in the 1960s I had to open a tin of chocolate-covered ants for a visiting dignitary. The chocolate provided a sweet contrast to the bitter taste of the ants' formic acid.
Keith Barratt-Smith, Hyde, Cheshire.

☐ My son bought canned earthquake for my daughter in Los Angeles.
Dennis Salt, Horsham, W. Sussex.

☐ I have a tin of alligator chowder from Florida.
M. J. Lyons, Lancing, W. Sussex.

☐ While living in North Carolina I discovered tinned pork brains in milk gravy; a true southern delicacy.
Dr Dave Richard, Pennsylvania.

☐ In my kitchen is a tin labelled 'Pacific Northwest Kitchen Sliced Slugs: Cajun Style, in Louisiana Hot Sauce', packed by Slyme Tyme Ltd of Newport, Oregon. I have not yet sampled the contents.
Lawrence Moran, Eugene, Oregon.

☐ In 1990 in Hungary, I bought two tins labelled 'The Last Breath of Communism'.
David Lewis, Ferney-Voltaire, France.

☐ Back in the 1960s, my teenage daughter came home with a tin of fried locusts. They were obviously genuine but too oily.
D. H. O'Dell, Hailsham, E. Sussex.

☐ I bought tins of 'Genuine London Fog' and 'Dehydrated Thames Water' (instructions: Just add water) near the Embankment many years ago.
A. Liebenthal, Pinner, Middlx.

QUESTION: Why a *red* carpet?

☐ The red carpet is an early crowd control measure. If a

dignitary was shot, the crowd would not be able to see
the blood, thus reducing panic.
Benjamin J. Elton, Manchester.

**QUESTION: Is it true that even a blind chameleon can
change its colour to that of its surroundings?**

☐ CHAMELEONS have dedicated a large area of brain to
vision. Each eye has colour, 3-D, 180-degree vision. And
many of the more than 100 chameleon species have the use
of their primitive pineal gland, or third eye, located behind
the 'forehead'. A tiny hole in the skull allows the detection
of light and heat, making a limited degree of colour change
theoretically possible. However, the stress of being blinded
will likely result in dark, 'stressed' colour, whatever the
background. Utterly dependent on eyesight to catch prey,
a blind chameleon will soon be a dead chameleon!
Ray Cimino, Irish Herpetological Society, Clontarf, Dublin.

**QUESTION: If PCs become as common in schools as
exercise books, will handwriting become obsolete?**

☐ MY HANDWRITING, being quite illegible even to me, is
already obsolete. I am word-processing this answer.
Meg Forrest, York.

☐ IN SAN FRANCISCO in 1970, none of my bosses could
do joined-up writing because they had been forced to type
everything from high school onwards; my own handwriting
was regarded as wonderful.
Ron Farquhar, Wimbledon, London SW19.

QUESTION: Have British farmers ever initiated any environmental or animal welfare reform without pressure by government?

☐ BRITISH farmers have taken the lead in many policy areas. To give just a few recent examples: the NFU helped frame the codes of welfare practice which now form the basis of UK legislation to protect animals; it obtained, through COPA (the European farmers' association), a commitment from EU ministers to review current EU welfare policies. The NFU was also instrumental in the reform of veal production in the UK in 1990, and brought pressure to bear for the 1997 review on the European veal-crate system to be brought forward. In 1992 the NFU report *Farming and the Environment* called for a voluntary scheme to allow farmers to contribute to maintaining the countryside. Last year the European Commission agreed to permit woodland to be planted on set-aside land, following intensive lobbying by the NFU and other organisations. The NFU has also cooperated with various environmental organisations – for example in co-hosting a conference with Friends of the Earth on the alternative use of crops and renewable forms of energy.
Sir David Naish, President, National Farmers' Union, London WC2.

☐ THE environmental impact of agricultural practices is so fundamental that there are very few examples left in the UK of true climax vegetation. Most 'landscapes' are the result of centuries and millennia of human endeavour. For example, the rolling South Downs, loved by many as 'countryside', are quite artificial – maintained only by farming, in the absence of which they would revert to thick impenetrable forest (but packed full of wildlife that has now all but disappeared – wild boars, bears, etc.). And the patchwork of fields and hedgerow so characteristic of the East Midlands, and so quintessentially English (with their

accompanying flora and fauna), are not only completely removed from the 'natural' environment but are also a relatively new addition to the landscape (following the Enclosure Acts of the 18th and 19th centuries).
Dr Julian Wiseman, Faculty of Agriculture and Food Sciences, University of Nottingham.

☐ ORGANIC farmers are unique in Britain in having voluntarily imposed restrictions on their enterprises for environmental reasons, without expecting hand-outs from the taxpayer. Apart from avoiding the use of pesticides, organic farmers are prohibited from removing hedgerows without prior consultation with the Soil Association, nor can they drain wetland areas of conservation value. So it's not surprising that a greater variety and number of birds are found on organic compared to chemical-using farms.
Robin Maynard, Soil Association, Bristol.

QUESTION: Muslim men in Islamic countries are able to have four wives. Assuming women make up roughly half the population, if only 25 per cent of Muslim men have four wives, then all the women are married. Does that mean that 75 per cent of men in Islamic countries are bachelors?

☐ THE questioner is mistaken in believing that Muslim men, in accordance with Islam, wed four wives *per se.* Islam recognises the spiritual, moral and social merits of a legal 'one-man-one-woman' relationship. The Holy Qur'an (the Last Testament of God) clearly states that monogamy is the ideal. Polygamy, though permitted, is rare and sanctioned as a last resort in helping to solve society's specific human problems – and *only* upon the free consent of the first wife. Allah, the Creator, sanctioned polygamy after an early battle was fought where many Muslim men,

who were slain and murdered, left behind widows and orphaned young daughters. Man was permitted to take a second wife (maximum four) in these circumstances. Islam will permit polygamy if the first wife is barren. Polygamy can solve the threat of desertion by the husband. Equally, the emotional burden on the first wife is lifted and her inability to reproduce is safely compensated. Polygamy is also allowed to avoid a husband committing adultery. Islam accepts the real problem of infidelity and offers a practical solution. Polygamy ensures that each wife's honour and dignity are secured, and the moral conduct of society remains intact.
A. Hussein, London.

QUESTION: What is the origin of the modern usage of the word 'gay'?

□ MELVILLE in *Moby Dick* (1851) uses 'gay' in its slang sense throughout, as he does 'fairy', 'queen' and 'queer'. They can't have been so understood by a mass audience – he wanted to sell books, not go to jail – but since he'd just been four years at sea, it's reasonable to suppose they were sailors' slang. The American whaling industry in which he'd served operated out of the Quaker strongholds of Nantucket and New Bedford. Somewhere in the writings of Bertrand Russell is a story about his first wife, the American Quakeress Alys. She used 'gay' as a disparaging term: to her, 'gay' was anything non-Quaker in lifestyle. Quakers, at least in the US, used it to connote vanity, ostentation, hedonism. Could it be that the sailors from this community, meeting a whole new lifestyle at sea, extended the word to mean something else their community would undoubtedly have despised?
Sheenagh Pugh, Canton, Cardiff.

□ FOR hundreds of years 'gay' referred to casual sex. It once described roués and prostitutes. Victorian rakes

didn't flock to Gay Paree because it was a jolly place.
Peter R. Brooke, Straloch, Aberdeen.

☐ MEMBERS of the Religious Society of Friends are familiar with the phrase 'gay Quaker' in its non-sexual sense – but the term Quakeress used by Sheenagh Pugh is rarely if ever used. For more than 300 years Quakers, recognising that all are equal in the sight of God, do not use titles, even Mr, Mrs, Miss or Ms. 'Quaker' derives from the verb to *quake* and has no gender: 'Quakeress' as a means of identifying women from men can only have come from outsiders who felt a need to identify gender.
John Dunning, Hoddesdon, Herts.

☐ THE usage derives from demonstrations in America in the early 1970s proclaiming homosexual equality. Demonstrators carried placards with the slogan 'Good As You'. The acronym GAY stuck.
Samantha Hannay, London.

☐ SAMANTHA HANNAY is wrong. In its meaning of loose-moralled, 'gay' goes back to the late Middle Ages; when it occurs in old ballads the lady in question is about to do something awful, like commit adultery. 'Dance over, my lady gay!', in 'London Bridge is Falling Down', is a straightforward reference to women involved in the same profession as the sad little waif in the *Punch* cartoon of the 1840s asking her downcast friend: 'Tell me, Maud, 'ow long 'ave you been gay?' The 1811 *Dictionary of the Vulgar Tongue* defines 'gaying instrument' as the penis. By the 19th century it had become linked to males with males.
John Brunner, South Petherton, Somerset.

QUESTION: Why do mosquitoes emit such an unpleasant high-pitched whine instead of stalking their victims silently?

□ THE whine is generated by a tiny computerised device in the ear canal known as a 'plimplim'. On detecting a flying insect in the vicinity, the plimplim activates a scanner located in the left elbow. This checks out whether or not the insect is a mosquito. If it is, the plimplim emits the whine as a warning. Mosquitoes in Sumatra are now believed to be working on a scrambler which interrupts the plimplim, rendering their prey utterly helpless.
Andrew P. McMillan, Glasgow.

□ THE sound is not emitted by a vocal organ but is a mechanical consequence of very rapid beating of the wings. In the female, which is the blood-feeding sex, the wings beat 400 times per second. Male mosquitoes, which do not feed on blood, beat their wings about twice as fast and locate females in a mating swarm by their lower wing beat frequency. Presumably mosquitoes could not evolve a means of flying with such agility without emitting an audible whine which sometimes allows potential victims to locate them in the dark and to take violent countermeasures.
C. F. Curtis and R. Williams, London School of Hygiene and Tropical Medicine, London WC1.

QUESTION: When ducks fly in a V-formation, is the duck at the apex the dominant bird?

□ THE duck at the apex, and similarly the leading bird in goose and swan skeins, is usually an older individual with greater experience in navigating – although during normal flight this tiring position is taken by a succession of birds. The V-formation is because ducks and other wildfowl have a curved upper-wing surface, creating lift. As this air passes the wing it produces a swirl effect and creates a backdraft which aids the flight of following birds on either side. The

V-shape is thus the most aerodynamic and energy-efficient form of flight.
David Probert, Wildlife & Wetlands Trust, Caerlaverock, Dumfriesshire.

QUESTION: When was the first vending machine used and what did it vend?

☐ A COIN-IN-THE-SLOT system was used in London during the early 19th century for selling newspapers – not so much a labour-saving device as an ingenious use of the principle that machines (unlike people) can't be punished for breaking the law. To discourage the spread of 'dangerous' ideas, information about parliamentary sleaze, etc., the Government imposed a hefty stamp duty on newspapers, which raised their price beyond the pockets of the masses. The tax was widely evaded, even though it was illegal to sell unstamped newspapers. One solution was the mechanical vendor. Customers entering the shop turned a pointer on a dial to indicate the journal they wanted and inserted their money. An unidentifiable operator concealed behind a screen then slid the paper down a chute to the customer. (See *Poor Men's Guardians* by Stanley Harrison, Lawrence & Wishart, 1974.)
Tom Watson, London N1.

☐ IN 215 BC, the mathematician Hero of Alexandria published a method of dispensing holy water through a coin-operated mechanism. The water was contained in a covered urn in which an upright rod balanced on one side a small plate, while on the other side a bell-shaped cap was suspended to fit over and close the water outlet from the urn. The position of the plate under a slit in the top of the urn ensured that when a coin was pushed through the

slit it dropped on to the plate, depressing it so as to lift
the cap on the other side. The outlet being thus opened,
the water flowed freely until the coin slid off the tipped
plate, sending the apparatus into reverse to stop the flow.
How much water the Egyptian worshipper received for the
money was a matter of chance and it is not known whether the
device was ever put into practice. In Britain it was not until
the 17th century that the first instance of automatic vending
was recorded. It was a device known as an honour box, for
dispensing snuff or tobacco, which was used in taverns and
held about 1lb (450 grams) of tobacco or the equivalent of
snuff. An old English halfpenny dropped in the slot and
triggered the opening of the spring-loaded lid, but the device
was less ingenious than Hero's, for unless the user closed
the box by hand, other customers could help themselves to
the contents without paying. (Source: *Automatic Vending
Machines*, Colin Emmins, Shire Publications.)
Janette Gledhill, Vend Inform, Banstead, Surrey.

**QUESTION: From 16 April my phone number has had
11 digits. The US has a much larger population but
their numbers are only 10 digits. Was BT's 'Phone
Day' really necessary?**

□ OBVIOUSLY the telephone number digits have to be
increased to keep up with telephone number salaries.
Peter Latarche, Bradford.

□ THE question is a little unfair to BT – the number
change has been imposed by Oftel. Numbers in the US
do not include the digit (in their case 1) which prefixes
long-distance calls, whereas our own include the initial 0.
So their numbers are the same length as ours became in
April 1995. Telephone numbering is not as simple as it first
appears. The area code, including the initial 0, comprises

four (soon to be five) digits outside the largest cities. Local numbers in these areas are normally allocated with first digits in the range 2 to 8, giving a theoretical capacity of 700,000, assuming all are six-digit numbers. However, the first one, two or three digits indicate which individual exchange the number is on. There are exchanges in the Highlands, the Lake District and rural Wales, with fewer than 100 lines but each needs its own discrete numbering range, leading to rapid exhaustion of the theoretical capacity. Additionally, numbers which are given up by one user are not available for immediate re-allocation, since the new user would be troubled by calls for the previous one. And the rapid growth of fax machines, mobile phones and premium-rate information services has led to an explosion in demand for numbers. Once the change has been implemented the problem should be solved for many years.

Bob Osborne, Ipswich, Suffolk.

QUESTION: What is the origin of the expression 'face the music'?

☐ AN EDICT of Cromwell's parliament forbade the use of the organ in churches and ordered their destruction. None remained at the time of the Restoration so musical instruments were used and galleries provided for instrumentalists. When hymns and psalms were sung, the congregation turned towards the gallery, 'facing the music'.

(Ms) B. Drew, London NW1.

QUESTION: Vampires, werewolves and the like are said to be active while there is a full moon. Why? Surely these beasties would prefer to do their worst when moonlight is at a minimum.

□ ONLY during the full moon can you see at night – and before there was street lighting, most potential victims would stay at home. The werewolf would risk bumping into things in the darkness – and werewolves were especially prone to injury. The likely origin of the werewolf legend, and its vampire variant, is an inherited disease called porphyria. The porphyrin ring is a vital component of haemoglobin which is vital in carrying oxygen round in our blood. It is also a pigment and the colours it produces are all seen in a bruise as it breaks down. Starting red, it is changed to a yellow-green compound also seen in bile. Porphyria sufferers can't break this compound down and recycle its iron. When the pigment gets into the skin the porphyric gets rashes and scars from sunlight acting on the pigment. The sufferer quickly learns to stay out of the sun. Tender, scarred faces are hard to shave and beards are often preferred. In addition, nails and teeth begin to stain reddish brown and may fall out. Eyes also may look red and victims readily become anaemic. This can, at least partially, be overcome by taking a diet rich in iron. The richest source known is blood. Finally, the abnormal porphyrins can cross into the brain and drive you mad. So an anaemic, hairy madman with red teeth and eyes, who avoids the sun, wandering around when he can see at night seeking to supplement his diet with blood is not too difficult to picture as the werewolf.
(Dr) Steve Seddon, Newcastle-under-Lyme, Staffs.

QUESTION: I know it tastes delicious, but why does Parmesan cheese smell like vomit?

□ THAT'S a relief. I was worried that my vomit smelled like Parmesan cheese.
Ian Payn (ian.payn@dga.co.uk)

☐ NOT all Parmesan cheese smells like vomit. Unlike the horrible stuff that supermarkets sell ready grated in cartons, Parmesan sold whole, and grated or sliced immediately prior to use, has no sour smell and tastes heavenly.
Judy Webb, London SW2.

QUESTION: What was grist and why was it milled?

☐ ANYONE who has drunk beer or whisky should be grateful that grist is still with us. It is the Old English term still used for malted barley that has been ground in a mill in order to extract sugars from the malt by mixing with hot water. The resulting fermentable liquid is also known by its Old English name – *wort* (pronounced 'wert').
Ken Maitland, Wine & Spirit Education Trust, London EC4.

☐ WHEAT differs according to variety, place of origin, growing season and harvesting conditions. The miller wishes to produce flour of a consistent baking quality. In order to achieve this, different types of wheat are blended and milled together in carefully calculated proportions. This mixture is technically known as the grist, and its nature will vary according to the type of flour being made. Sometimes, when a poor season has produced an inferior local crop of wheat, the situation may be saved by mixing into the grist a proportion of expensive imported wheat. Hence the expression: 'It's all grist to the mill.' The miller's skill lies in maintaining consistency of product while still making a profit.
Charles Bather, Colchester, Essex.

QUESTION: Given (a) the velocity of a falling object,

(b) the average individual's reaction time and (c) the speed of sound, is there any point in shouting a warning to those below if I accidentally drop a heavy object from a tall structure?

☐ FORGETTING about air resistance, the basic difference between the progress of your shout and the heavy object is that the object accelerates progressively, while the shout travels at a constant (though high) speed. If you drop the object from a height of 10 metres and shout immediately, the person has almost a second to get out of the way, increasing to about three seconds if the building you drop the object from is 100 metres high. Eventually, however, the object has long enough to accelerate past your shout, giving the victim no chance to respond, which happens when your building is about 900 metres tall. In that case, you'd best spend the intervening few seconds covering your tracks and preparing an alibi for the unlikely event that the victim survives and decides to sue.
(Dr) Simon Saunders, Cambridge.

☐ DR SAUNDERS seems to have his numbers in a twist. Assuming a temperature of around 18°C so that sound travels at a constant speed of 342 m/s; that the acceleration due to gravity is 9.81 m/s^2; that air resistance can be ignored; that the sound travels unimpeded and is still audible when it reaches the person; then the optimal height of the building is 5.96 km. This is the height that maximises the time between the arrival of the sound and the object, with the time interval being 17.4 seconds (should be enough for the slowest of reactions). For heights up to around 23.8 km the sound will reach the person before the object. Absurd, perhaps, but that's assumptions for you.
Charles Arthurs, Painswick, Glos.

☐ DR SAUNDERS began his reply: 'Forgetting about air

resistance . . .' You can't in this case. Air resistance increases as a falling body's speed increases, eventually equalling the gravitational force. Thereafter, the body will fall at a constant velocity, the terminal velocity. This final velocity depends on the shape and density of the object. Drop a feather from a height and it will reach a very low terminal velocity. Even for objects likely to do serious damage to those below, the terminal velocity will always be far less than the speed of sound.
(Dr) Stephen J. Moss, Sutton Coldfield, W. Midlands.

QUESTION: Why is Shropshire sometimes referred to as 'Salop'?

☐ THE county town of Shropshire is Shrewsbury. The oldest recorded spelling is 'Scrobbesbyrig', meaning 'the fortified town near the place which is known as the Scrub'. When William the Conqueror sent his French clerks around the country, they found difficulty pronouncing the name. To make it easier they changed the 'c' to an 'a' and then, because the French lisped, the 'r' became an 'l' (as in Salisbury instead of Sarisbury). There are documents from shortly after the Norman conquest which refer to the town as 'Salopsberie'.
H. F. Moxon, Bury, Lancs.

QUESTION: With what tune did the Pied Piper lure the rats from Hamlyn?

☐ WITHOUT knowing the exact strain of rats in Hamlyn, it is not possible to determine the tune to any degree of certainty. However, the Common Blue rat, or *Rattus sleazius*, can be seen attracted in large numbers by the strains of 'Land of Hope and Glory'.
Alan Perrow, Embsay, Yorks.

☐ THE Pied Piper was playing the score to the lyric: 'I am going to lay down my burden down by the riverside.'
Arthur Howden, Nelson, Lancs.

QUESTION: I want to dominate the world. I have thought of becoming the head of a multinational computer software conglomerate and buying out my competitors. Are there any better alternatives?

☐ DERIVATIVES. Bar(r)ing any problems, that is.
Simon Walsh, Braintree, Essex.

☐ SIMPLY set up a base (preferably underground) on a volcanic island, steal a couple of space shuttles and a few intercontinental ballistic missiles (optional), find yourself a nubile nymphette of a mistress and perhaps a pet shark/cat/Rottweiler and you will have definitely taken a step in the right direction. One piece of advice. Should any secret agents come snooping around your island do not: 1. leave them unattended to die in a Heath Robinson-style contraption. 2. be tempted to display your cunning by revealing all the details of your plans to them.
Sabbi Lall, Oxford.

☐ BECOME a New Man. The hand that rocks the cradle rules the world.
Janet Evans, Ascott-under-Wychwood, Oxon.

☐ START by inheriting a family newspaper business, preferably in Australia. Buy up every other overseas newspaper you can. Give yourself a terrific profit base by sacking anyone remotely connected with journalism. Then start buying TV stations. All will eventually be at

your beck and call. And put the transmitters up in space, so no one can get at them.
Tim Myers, Upton Park, London E13.

QUESTION: Is going off at a tangent the best antidote to a circular argument?

☐ IT DEPENDS to what degree the tangent is relevant.
Douglas Newton, Sheffield.

QUESTION: How did the ancient Romans calculate with their Roman numerals? Am I right in thinking that they could neither multiply nor divide?

☐ ADDITION and subtraction are fairly straightforward, but multiplication and division are more difficult and I can only find one author who addresses the problem – Lancelot Hogben, in his book for children *Man Must Measure: The Wonderful World of Mathematics.* He says: 'We rightly think of the Romans as a nation of conquerors, but they were never able to conquer the art of calculating as we know it today. Even simple multiplication was a slow and space-consuming process. The Roman merchant might use numerals for recording, but calculating was still a task for the slave working with an abacus.' Hogben then gives an illustration of 123 x 165 in Roman numerals, too space-consuming for these columns.
Bill Williams, life fellow, University of Leeds.

☐ THE Romans surmounted their problems in calculation with the aid of the abacus, which appears to have been in use in Egypt by about 500 BC. The symbol for zero, essential to modern numerical notation, seems to have been suggested by an Indian mathematician in about AD

500 and picked up by the Arabs about 200 years later. The first book, by an Arab, using positional notation came in about AD 810. I have seen shopkeepers in the Central Asian Republics of the old Soviet Union using an abacus with a similar speed to some of our own shop assistants using a pocket calculator. (Source: I. Asimov, *Chronology of Science and Discovery*.)
Bryn Giles, Henleaze, Bristol.

QUESTION: Why do men's and women's conveniences so often contain the same number of (seated) toilets while demand is obviously unequal?

☐ THE unequal number of seated toilets in public conveniences probably dates from the days when women both travelled and drank less than men. A bill to equalise this facility, presented by Cardiff Central MP Jon Owen Jones, is unlikely to gain an early second reading in Parliament. This Public Conveniences (No. 2) Bill would require each local authority to ensure that no less than one lavatory for women is provided per 550 women and female children, and per 1,100 men and male children, known to be dwelling in the area. Lavatories for men may be in the form of a bowl within a cubicle or urinal, provided that the former shall consist of not less than a third of the lavatories provided for men. The apparent bias towards women in this formula arises from observations that women require twice as long to urinate as do men.
Allan Horsfall, Coordinator, Convenience, Manchester.

QUESTION: What was the subject of Dr Ian Paisley's doctoral thesis?

☐ THERE was no thesis. According to the book *Paisley* by

Ed Maloney and Andy Pollok (Poolbeg Press) he has two doctorates, both honorary. His first was given in 1954 by the Pioneer Theological Seminary in Rockford, Illinois; this was after he had paid $25 for a BA he had taken on a correspondence course. Seminaries such as the one at Rockford are commonly known as 'degree mills'. In 1966 – the year Paisley served three months in jail for illegal assembly – Bob Jones Jr gave Paisley his second honorary doctorate in recognition of his 'prison martyrdom'.
John Crowley, South Harrow, Middlx.

QUESTION: I had a question to ask Notes & Queries but have forgotten it. Can anybody tell me what it was?

☐ I HAVE written an answer to the question but have forgotten to include it in this letter.
L. J. Bailey, Porth, Mid Glamorgan.

☐ YOU actually had two questions. The answers are: Jeffrey Archer and amnesia.
David S. Collins, Harpenden, Herts.

☐ Is THIS the question?
T. J. Halj, Manchester.

QUESTION: Can a magnetic tape (such as video cassette) be wiped clean if it comes too close to a large magnet (in a loudspeaker, for example)?

☐ IN 1990 I worked in the computer room of a steel mill in Ohio. One of the technicians was asked to clear a computer tape. Instead of using the standard computer program to do this, he took it outside the computer room, out on to

the mill, and signalled to the driver of one of the overhead cranes. The crane driver lowered the giant electro-magnet, used for lifting scrap steel off the line, and the technician waved the tape underneath. We were horrified. Not so much for the technician putting himself in danger from falling scrap, as for the computer tape, which was being waved around in a dirty, wet, corrosive environment. We refused to let him try out the tape on the computer. Undeterred by his telling off, the technician tried the experiment again, with another tape, this time wrapped in a plastic bag. It worked, but I don't recommend it.
Mike Frost, Bilton, Rugby, War.

☐ A 400 Tesla superconducting magnet I once worked with wiped out cassette tapes at a range of about 30 cm. Loudspeaker magnets are generally weaker but will damage tape at a close enough range. In practice you would be unlucky to wipe a tape accidentally as the cabinet should prevent the tape from coming too close to the magnet.
Matt Lowy, Ascot, Berks.

QUESTION: Which has been the most uneventful day of recent times?

☐ TWENTY-NINTH February 1995.
Simon Walsh, Braintree, Essex.

☐ LATE in 1994, Bridgwater must have had a quiet time, since the local paper had a column headlined: 'No more human remains found.'
Paul Bovett, Bridgwater, Somerset.

☐ SOME years ago the South African Broadcasting Corporation reported: 'There is no news tonight.'
Gertrude Cohn, London NW3.

☐ LET us consider that there is such a day. Then we can be sure that on that day, a not insignificant thing occurred: it became the most uneventful day of recent times. Now this is probably enough for the said day not to be the most uneventful day of recent times. So if there is such a day, then it isn't. Hope this makes things clear.
Felix Salmon, London SE19.

QUESTION: Why do washing machines have windows?

☐ THIS is all part of Microsoft's plan to take over the world. Having conquered the world of personal computers, they are now moving to take over your utility rooms and kitchens. Watch out for Windows™ appearing on kettles and toasters.
Paul Beckett, Wokingham, Berks.

☐ I HAVE two cats which sit in front of the washing machine and tap at the window as clothes spin past. From their total absorption in this mindless activity, I can only surmise that it is the feline equivalent of a computer game.
Oliver Thornton, Crowborough, E. Sussex.

☐ IT IS so that you can panic when pinky suds reveal that you accidentally put a cheap red T-shirt in with your lovely white cotton shirts.
Hazel Sydeserff, Edinburgh.

QUESTION: Why are paste diamonds so called?

☐ PASTE diamonds are imitations, often made from glass to which lead has been added. Although this increases the brilliance of the glass, it also reduces its hardness. My *Jewelers' Dictionary* (1945) says the word 'comes from *pasta*, Italian for food, in allusion to its plastic nature'. Compared to diamond, the hardest substance known to man, glass is indeed soft and plastic.
Anthony Morland, Geneva.

QUESTION: Does anyone ever cut the grass on the motorway verges?

☐ ONLY a small part is cut. This is a strip 1.2 metres wide along the edge of the carriageway which acts as a refuge for stranded motorists or creates visibility areas in front of junctions, signs and signals. Some cutting is done in areas where wild flowers are sown or planted, to encourage seeding and maintain an attractive and diverse flora. Beyond the mown areas the verges are a valuable habitat for our native flora.
Nigel Organ, Head of Road Engineering and Environment, Highways Engineering, London SE1.

QUESTION: What does OK stand for? Why is it such an internationally understood phrase?

☐ OK's origins are still hotly debated by American professors. Bill Bryson, in his book *Made in American*, lists nine possible derivations, ranging from Only Kissing to Olla Kalla – allegedly the Greek for all good – to *okeh*, the Choctaw Indian word for Yes. Some claim that OK was what President Andrew Jackson, who started life in the backwoods of Tennessee, wrote in the margins of documents signifying Orl Korect when he was in the

White House in the 1830s. The initials first appeared in print in the *Boston Morning Post* in 1839 as a whimsical shortening of Oll Korrect and were taken up the following year by supporters of Jackson's protégé and successor as president, Martin Van Buren, who set up OK Clubs to help his election prospects. Van Buren was known as Old Kinderhook, after his home town in New York, but that may have been a piece of tidying-up to improve the nickname of a rather fastidious politician.
Steve Bates, London SW1.

☐ ONE theory is that it originated among African Americans. Apparently, in Mandingo *o ke* means 'all right' and in Wolof (Senegal) *wav kay* means 'yes indeed'. Use of the term in New England circa 1840 (the first known use was in a Boston newspaper) has been put down to the steady influx of refugees from the Southern slave states. Other suggestions about origins include: the Latin *omnia corrects*; the Southern French dialect word *oc (oui)*; *aux quais* ('to the harbour') stencilled on casks of Puerto Rico rum specially selected for export; Aux Cayes (a place in Haiti noted for the excellence of its rum); the Scots 'och aye'; and the initials of Otto Kaiser (a German-born US industrialist).
Basil Morgan, Uppingham, Rutland.

☐ IT GOES back much further than either of your correspondents suggest. When the Black Prince married Eleanor of Aquitaine, he became Henri II of France (which was in fact four different countries in those days). The local dialect of Aquitaine (the south-west of France) was Occitaine – it's still spoken today in more rural parts. 'Oc' is obviously a shortened form of Occitaine and also means 'yes'. Henri brought this word back to England and the rest is history.
Dave Novell, Leeds.

☐ DAVE NOVELL'S letter contains historical inaccuracies. First, the Black Prince may have been Duke of Aquitaine (or Guyenne as it was known to the English) but he did not marry Eleanor of Aquitaine – he was Eleanor's great-great-great-great-grandson. Eleanor's husband became Henry II of England, but Henri II of France was the husband of Catherine de Medici and died in a tournament in 1559. France was never four different countries, just one country whose king was so weak that he had magnates who were more powerful than he. Occitaine was never a dialect but a full language, spoken widely across all of what is now southern France, north-east Spain, the Balearics and north-west Italy. From Occitaine are descended Provençal, Mallorquin and Catalan. The great linguistic divide of France was typified by the word used for 'yes'. In the north it was *oeuil*, which has now become *oui* but was then pronounced something like 'aye'. In the south 'yes' was *oc*, hence the alternative name of the heartland of Occitaine – Languedoc. But, if we are genuinely to believe that 'oc' was the origin of the term 'OK', it has even older roots than Mr Novell suggests. 'Oc' itself was derived from the Latin affirmative *hoc*.
Colin Pilkington, Ormskirk, Lancs.

QUESTION: How can the smell of damp be obliterated? We had a minor flood during a recent downpour and, while new carpets have eliminated the smell of cabbages from our lives, the dank, sweet, methane-laden scent still permeates out of the understair basement cupboard despite liberal applications of Domestos.

☐ A TIME-honoured method of obliterating unpleasant smells is to fumigate with burning brown paper.
R. J. Ellis, Dowland, Devon.

QUESTION: Where does the fibre for All-Bran come from and what happens to the rest of whatever plant it is?

☐ FROM wheat bran, one of the richest sources of fibre. Bran is removed from the outer layers of wheat grains as they are milled to produce flour.
Dr I. P. Bell, Kellogg's, Manchester.

QUESTION: In the new South Africa there is suddenly an abundance of 'nations': Afrikaner nation, Zulu nation, Xhosa nation, etc. What are the criteria for calling a group of people a 'nation'?

☐ A NATION exists when there is a general consensus among its 'members' that they share a common identity – be it language, culture or a claim to a geographical area (a 'state' or a desire to form one). In times of oppression, for example under apartheid in South Africa, different groups of people will band together to challenge their common oppressor. So with the dismantling of apartheid, new 'nations' appear as cultural groups re-discover their affinities and claims to land.
Rupert Smith, Liverpool 8.

☐ THE answer may be subtler than Rupert Smith suggests. It is true that all nations include a 'claim to land' within their self-definitions. But a nation *as a group of people* is quite distinct from a 'nation-state', which may be defined as a culturally homogenous group living within a clearly demarcated territory. Nations without land are held together by their literature, their art and their particular interpretation of history. Thus, as Benedict Anderson suggests, nations are perhaps best defined as 'communities of the imagination'.
John W. Wylie, Rusholme, Manchester.

□ THE question itself exhibits one of the more notorious criteria – the imposition of 'nationhood' on others by a powerful sub-group for underhand reasons. There was not 'suddenly' a variety of alleged nations in South Africa after 1990. A quarter-century ago, as part of the fraudulent 'homelands' sophistry, the white minority regime's propagandists started calling the various tribal groups in South Africa 'nations'. Thus, in a speech to the UN Security Council in October 1974, Pretoria's 'Pik' Botha referred to apartheid as 'multinational development'. The South African concept of 'nations' being based on apartheid remains divisive.

Len Clarke, Uxbridge, Middlx.

□ 'A NATION is a historically evolved, stable community of language, territory, economic life, and psychological make-up manifested in a community of culture . . . None of the above characteristics is by itself sufficient to define a nation' (Joseph Stalin, *Marxism and the National Question*, 1912). Liberal theory gives high importance to the right of such social entities to 'self-determination'. By that it usually emphasises the right to secede from other social entities and ignores the cost of mutual hatred between different communities and nations. The Marxist tradition emphasises that possible modes of self-determination also include the right to federate with other nations or to merge with them in a unitary state. The right to union is thus defined as at least as important as the right to secession. The fact that nations usually include within their borders members and communities of other nations thus becomes less of a basic problem for the theory of national self-determination. In Marxism for this and other, specifically socialist, reasons, unionist modes are in principle at least as valid as secessionist, nationalistic modes.

B. R. Cosin, London NW3.

QUESTION: Has anyone ever survived an air crash by using the equipment demonstrated by cabin crew at the start of each flight?

☐ IT DEPENDS what you mean by crash. But the following recent non-fatal accidents would suggest that it is worth paying attention. A DC-9 landing at Vigo, Spain, hit the approach lights, landed short of the runway, the undercarriage collapsed and the aircraft caught fire (passengers saved by emergency exits and evacuation slides); a Boeing 747 overran the runway on landing at Hong Kong and ended in the sea (life jackets); 19 passengers were injured when a MD-82 encountered clear air turbulence (seat belts).
Vic Smith, Ickenham, Middlx.

☐ ON 28 April 1988, a Boeing 737 lost a large section of its fuselage roof at 24,000 feet as the result of metal fatigue. One of the cabin crew, whose duties prevented her being strapped in, was swept away. She was the only fatality. The 89 passengers were all wearing seat belts, and survived.
Timothy Lidbetter, Kingston upon Thames, Surrey.

QUESTION: My brother lives in England and I live in New Zealand. Do we see the moon the same way up?

☐ TO HAVE the same view as his brother, the questioner should stand on his head. It is rather disconcerting, after travelling to the other hemisphere, to see the figure of a familiar constellation such as Orion appear upside down. What is even more disorientating is that things move across the sky in the opposite direction. The sun appears in New Zealand to move from right to left as one faces north; in England from left to right as one faces south.

William Somerville, Department of Physics and Astronomy, University College London.

☐ WHEN I first came to Britain from New Zealand, I was disturbed to find that the moon was upside down. It is easy to prove that the Northern Hemisphere orientation is the incorrect one. In the Southern Hemisphere the moon makes a C when it is increasing and a D when it is Decreasing. In the Northern Hemisphere the letters are the wrong way round. Indeed, an Italian proverb calls the moon a liar for this very reason.

Ian Dunbar, Warrington.

☐ I AM sorry to learn from my countryman Ian Dunbar that the moon is a liar according to an Italian proverb. It is only trying to be helpful to German speakers, for whom the crescent forms a (handwritten) 'a' and a (handwritten) 'z'. 'A' stands for *abnehmend* ('waning') and 'z' for *zunehmend* ('waxing'). No doubt very confusing for Germans who emigrated to the southern hemisphere.

D. A. Pashby, Woodford Green, Essex.

☐ HERE in the northern hemisphere its crescent matches those in the French words *premier* and *dernier*, for first and last quarter.

John Wymer, Bridport, Dorset.

QUESTION: Do Germany's autobahns have a higher or lower accident rate than British motorways?

☐ SINCE the systems for reporting road accidents vary from country to country, the most reliable comparison is by looking solely at the number of road accident

deaths. OECD statistics show that the number of fatalities per vehicle-kilometre travelled on German autobahns is approximately twice that on British motorways. The rate on autobahns in the former West Germany is about 50 per cent higher than in Britain.
Jeremy Grove, Road Accident Statistics Branch, Department of Transport, London SW1.

QUESTION: Is it possible to 'recover', through hypnosis or other means, a foreign language learnt as a child and subsequently forgotten?

☐ AT ONE of my parents' parties a friend of my younger brother, who was about 17 at the time, got very drunk and fell into a deep sleep on the bathroom floor. This boy had been brought up in Wales until the age of six or seven but spoke no Welsh. When I went to check on him later in the evening, he sat straight up, said two or three sentences of what sounded extremely like Welsh and then fell asleep again. He had no memory of this the following day. Unfortunately, I don't speak Welsh so I don't know if it was accurate, but it did sound very convincing!
Morag Christie, Forest Fields, Nottingham.

QUESTION: Do solicitors charge for time spent preparing their bills?

☐ THE answer will cost £50 plus VAT.
Donald G. Carrick, solicitor, Beverley, N. Humberside.

☐ SOLICITORS can charge for anything they like. They even make a − quite legal − charge for doing precisely nothing. The argument goes that while they are driving to work, going to the loo, etc., they are constantly thinking

about the cases they are working on. This time has a value. It even has a name. It's called 'a duty of care' (not 'a right con') and appears on invoices. I would like all tradesmen to adopt the same policy when doing work for solicitors. The plumber can quite legitimately charge for 'thinking about your ball cock, mate'.
Robert W. Colwell, Isleworth, Middlx.

QUESTION: Who invented the disco, and how did it occur to him or her?

☐ A STRONG contender must be Ron Diggins from Boston in Lincolnshire. As a young apprentice radio engineer in the 1930s, part of his job was to set up and operate public address equipment at various functions. By the mid-1940s he had started playing records at local dances, using wind-up gramophones and cumbersome 12-watt panatropes (amplifiers). It was from his constant attempts to improve and innovate that the first 'Diggola' hit the road in 1947. This pioneering machine had twin turntables, amplifier and speakers encased in a glittering console – still the basis of most disco equipment today. Ron estimates that he and his Diggola have appeared at some 20,000 dances, parties and other events at more than 700 different venues. Now aged 77, he still plays regularly in the Boston, Sleaford and Skegness area.
Bob Neish, Boston, Lincs.

☐ THE French *bibliothèque* (derived from the Greek for 'bookcase') first appeared in 1493, meaning a collection of books. *Discothèque* first appears in 1932, meaning a collection of gramophone records, or record library – then as a place where one could go to listen to records and, later, to dance.
T. J. Alford, Edgware, Middlx.

QUESTION: Is it an offence to open somebody else's Electronic Mail?

☐ YOU can't open e-mail at all, it just exists as a file on one or more hard disks. With ordinary letters, the envelope has a physical presence and can be somebody's property. If another person opens it they are interfering with private property. The same is not true of e-mail. However, it is illegal to attempt to gain access to a computer system that you are unauthorised to use, and this step is almost always necessary to read another's e-mail. The important exception is the case of the sysadmins on your local system. In their capacity as the maintainers of the system they are able to read any file, quite legally. It is generally considered foolish to send private material via e-mail, just one reason why pen and ink will be with us for a while yet. In any event, check with your sysadmin to find out the policy regarding private e-mail; it is at their discretion.
J. Peterson, University College London.

☐ J. PETERSON states that one can't open e-mail, since it just exists on a hard disk. But when a file is read on a computer system, one actually says that the file is 'opened', and this is the electronic equivalent of opening an envelope to read a letter. Computer-readable files containing personal data are strictly protected under the Data Protection Act 1984. I disagree with his statement that it is 'generally considered foolish to send private material via e-mail'. Many people throughout the world nowadays routinely protect their e-mail by means of extremely secure public-key encryption. This provides a secure 'envelope' for e-mail over an insecure communication channel.
Dr N. M. Queen, School of Mathematics & Statistics, University of Birmingham.

QUESTION: Why is washing-up liquid generally green?

□ IN THE early 1970s, the company I was working for completed a series of consumer tests. They took packets of identical standard white detergent and added 'speckles' of different colours – green, blue, red. The consumer panel was asked to rate the detergents and make comments. It rated the green spiked powders as mild, the blue with phrases such as 'firm but fair' and the red with criticism such as 'damaging and caustic'. Washing-up liquids are green to go with the claims that they are 'kind to the hands'. In further tests, this time on food products, I attended a panel to test the effect of colour on crisps preference. It was conducted in controlled lighting for the tasting and only when the lights came on again was it possible to see the crisps' colour. One panel, after rating the flavour of a particular product as being rather sweet, found that the crisps were blue. Several of the tasters were sick.
Mike Woods, Shipley, W. Yorks.

□ PROBABLY because Fairy Liquid, brand leader for the last 35 years, is green. Green was always the colour of the Fairy brands, starting with Fairy soap, launched in Newcastle upon Tyne in 1898.
Alison Hartley, Proctor & Gamble, Newcastle upon Tyne.

QUESTION: When, and why, did men first start shaving? At face value, it seems ludicrous to scrape hair off the body every day.

□ ALEXANDER THE GREAT is responsible. The rationale behind its introduction was that an enemy soldier could gain an advantage by seizing his opponent by the beard. I don't know if there are any records of soldiers being killed in this way in Classical times. Mary Renault, in her book *The Nature of Alexander*, suggests that his real motive was

to preserve his own androgynous appearance; the practice then spread to his men.
Alan Dimes, London SW10.

☐ THEY started long before Alexander the Great. He lived in the 4th century BC, but sculptures from the ancient civilisations of Mesopotamia, the Nile and the Indus show that members of the Sumerian, Egyptian and Indian ruling classes were clean-shaven 2,000–3,000 years earlier.
Nicolas Walter, London N1.

QUESTION: Everyone can observe the effects of the curvature of the earth by watching ships disappearing over the horizon. Is there any evidence that, far before science established that the earth was round, sailors had already stumbled on the truth?

☐ THE presence of crow's nests on ships suggests that sailors were certainly aware that increasing their height above sea level allowed them to see much further. In fact, the distance of the horizon is approximately proportional to the square root of the height above sea level. There is, however, a more direct way to establish that the earth is round. Given sufficient height, the earth's curvature is immediately apparent, as is evidenced by pictures from space. From experiments in our laboratory, we would predict that, at a height of 1 km (approximately 3,280 feet) looking out to sea, the curvature of the earth should just be detectable. Perhaps individuals in suitable geographical locations may be able to confirm this?
Dr David Whitaker, Department of Optometry, University of Bradford.

☐ THE question assumes that, at some time before modern science (the Dark Ages?), everyone believed the earth was

flat. So far as the evidence goes there never was such a time. It is probable that most people, well aware of such things as horizon phenomena and perhaps, too, the circular shadow cast on the moon by the earth during eclipses, believed the earth was round. Aristotle demonstrated this and Eratosthenes calculated the diameter and circumference correctly. Posidonius of Apamea repeated the experiment and miscalculated, thus causing Columbus (1,600 years later) to believe the westward route to Asia would be a shortcut. He was not worried whether he might sail over the edge! Why is it thought that so many people believed the earth was flat? Marjorie Nicolson, in *Mountain Gloom and Mountain Glory*, speculated that this may have arisen out of misunderstanding of disputes over whether the earth was originally *plana*, i.e. smooth, and that great mountains and depths were the result of God's curse and catastrophes like the Flood.
Dudley Knowles, University of Glasgow.

QUESTION: What exactly is the British institution called 'Liveries'?

☐ THESE are the Livery Companies of the City of London, of which there are now nearly 100. The older Livery companies are the descendants of the various guilds that regulated trades and crafts in the Middle Ages. Livery companies now have national memberships totalling around 16,000, forming a network of industrial achievers, the privileged and the well-connected. Research suggests that Livery companies were directly involved in founding modern freemasonry in the early 18th century, to help defend civic stability and mercantile interests throughout the country. The Grand Lodge of England was set up within the City of London in 1717 and for a number of years met at various City Livery company halls.
John Whitehead, Barbican, London EC2.

QUESTION: Why do the French count *soixante-dix, quatre vingts* **and** *quatre-vingt-dix* **instead of** *septante, octante* **and** *nonante?*

□ THIS method of counting is known as virgesimal, i.e. in twenties, and is not unique to French – Mayan and Welsh are other examples. It is believed that French uses this system as a relic of its Celtic predecessor. Twenty was probably chosen as a base rather than ten because the people who spoke these tongues were barefoot, and therefore counted on their toes as well as their fingers. In one language using the virgesimal system, the word for twenty is the same as that for human – that is, an entire human being had been used up in the count.
Mark Ure, Leicester.

QUESTION: Why is it that to make the poor work harder you pay them less, but to make the rich work harder you pay them more?

□ PAYING people more only makes them work harder if the *extra* pay satisfies some need. The poor *may* work harder if they have a job in which pay is related to output, because they have a real need for more money. Paying the poor less will only make them work harder under very restricted circumstances, which would include having a job to work at. No increase in pay can have any effect on how hard the unemployed work at job-seeking, but given that there are no jobs for most of them, increases in allowances would have other beneficial effects. Paying the rich more in order to make them work harder is also a myth. The rich also work harder only if the *extra* pay satisfies some need. In their case the need may be related to self-esteem, or job security, and the extra pay is really only a symbol of their worth. In some organisations, cheaper methods of keeping the bosses working, by overt recognition of their worth, are available: in the Royal Navy a row of gold oak leaves on your hat, or gradually increasing numbers of gold rings on your sleeve. Sadly, the pincer movement of trade unionism and Tory materialism have gone a long way towards destroying our perceptions of the complex nature of work motivation, reducing it to the single factor of cash.

J. J. W. Atkinson, Cleveland county councillor (Liberal Democrat), Stockton-on-Tees.

QUESTION: When will the Age of Aquarius start? I want to know if I'll be around to enjoy the party.

□ THE earth spins on its polar axis with a slight wobble, producing the Precession of the Equinoxes, which takes approximately 25,725 years. In astrological terms this 'Great Year' is divided into 12 'Great Months' or Ages, which are named after the signs of the zodiac. Each age is approximately 2,160 years and is characterised by appropriate attributes according to the sign involved. Aquarius 'rules' innovation, science, electronics, aviation, cooperation, television, advanced ideas, humanitarian objectives, idealism, exploration, revolution, etc. There have been many attempts to pinpoint the beginning of the Age of Aquarius but the modern consensus is that there is a gradual transition, lasting for several years. And typical manifestations of this period are now with us, including increased geophysical activity; escalation of armed conflict; a new spiritual awareness; and accelerated scientific and technological innovation.

Kenneth Woodward, Wrexham, Clwyd.

QUESTION: How do I know whether my pain threshold is low or high?

□ UNDER anaesthesia, where one must presume that emotional considerations have been switched off, the level of response to pain varies considerably between people and times. The body makes its own painkiller, endorphin, which acts in the spine and brain blocking the relaying of pain information. At any one time both the number of sites which can be blocked with endorphins, and the number blocked, can vary considerably. Thus the pain felt from a given stimulus will not be felt the same by different people, or by the same person at different times. People can learn to resist pain, altering their endorphin level subconsciously to do so. Hypnosis and acupuncture can induce endorphin production, as can high emotion and determination. Ultimately, you can only decide if your pain threshold is high or low by how much you respond to pain compared to those around you. If you decide to raise it, real determination is needed.
Dr Steve Seddon, Newcastle-under-Lyme, Staffs.

QUESTION: Given that the earth's surface has a decelerating effect on wind, why do lower clouds fly by faster than the higher ones?

□ THE reduction in wind speed near the surface has no real bearing on the subject. Perspective governs the apparent motion of the clouds, similar to sitting in a fast-moving train or car and seeing close objects moving past faster than ones further away. Clouds move at different speeds, and speeds generally increase with height, although not exclusively so. Just to complicate matters, clouds can also move in different directions at different heights. Interesting effects can be seen if clouds are observed

from a train or car (but don't try if you are the driver).
Malcolm Brooks, Met Office, Bracknell, Berks.

QUESTION: Who was Ralph Nader and what was his claim to fame?

☐ RALPH NADER, born 1934, was a comstocking American puritan whose innate aversion to alcohol, tobacco, sex and popular entertainment blossomed into an antipathy to almost everything humans could consume. Especially sugar. His book *Unsafe at any Speed*, an exposé of the lack of safety precautions of US cars in general and the Corvair in particular, sold half a million; his law suit against General Motors for launching a dirty tricks campaign against him made him a household name. Though a notoriously boring and graceless public speaker, he used this public platform to invent the college big money lecture circuit, inveighing against everything from food additives and sugar to Union Carbide and the banking system. Nascent ecologists cheered him and his message before driving home in their massive, gas-guzzling Chryslers and filling their bodies with 'poison'. He declined to run for President when proposed by Gore Vidal.
Chris Carmichael, South Gosforth, Newcastle upon Tyne.

QUESTION: Economists and politicians tell us that it is becoming more difficult to support the increasing proportion of pensioners. On the other hand we are encouraged to stay healthy in order to extend our life expectancy. Is this wise advice?

☐ AT ONE time, half the population was under 15 and the adult female quarter was running households rather than earning wages outside the home. Society was supported by the wages of the adult male quarter of the population. Society could again support higher dependency ratios. Tories currently prefer that this be through private sector arrangements, but this is an argument in moral dogmatics and not a question of our society's economic capability. The OAP-driven rise of the dependent sector is a red herring to aggravate regressive taxation. There was no outcry at the expansion of dependency at the youth end of society when compulsory schooling was raised from 14 to 16; or when the post-16 education sector trebled in a generation. Pensioners create jobs in the care sector; sustain jobs by spending on grocery, clothing and their quarterly bills; and create financial jobs as people start saving earlier with a view to a long retirement. At the young end of the scale, education, both further and nursery, creates jobs and lets women enjoy careers and independence, so expanding the pool and range of talent available to society.

F. D. Adam, Prestwich, Manchester.

QUESTION: When and where did we start crossing our fingers for luck?

□ CHRISTIANITY is probably responsible, given that the cross is its international symbol. Presumably it is a corruption of crossing your heart during prayer, which is essentially wishing for good luck.

Daryl Kayes, Binley, Coventry.

QUESTION: What is the most (monetarily) valuable object in the known universe in terms of value per unit mass?

□ A SUBSTANCE known as Prostaglandin E2 (used in

research into respiratory function) is commercially available at a cost of £17.90 per nanogram. This equates to £3,580 billion per kilogram.
John Peacock, Cardiff.

☐ *THE GUINNESS BOOK OF RECORDS* tells us that, in 1970, the element californium was available for sale at $10 per microgram, approximately £6 billion a kilo. Of course, it's unlikely you could buy a whole kilogram, but if you did you'd probably get a bulk discount.
Mike Frost, Bilton, Rugby.

☐ ATOMS much heavier than uranium do not occur in nature, and have to be made artificially in large accelerators. For the very heaviest elements, literally only a few atoms have been made, with the almost unimaginably small mass of about 0.00000000000000000000002 of a gram per atom. Considering the size of the accelerator and the length of time the scientific teams have worked on it, a million pounds would be a very conservative estimate of their cost, so these atoms are at least five thousand million million million million pounds per gram. This enormously exceeds the annual gross domestic product of the entire world. They only last a tiny fraction of a second before decaying, and for some of them a few grams in one place would cause a nuclear explosion. So if you can afford the price, the enjoyment will be short-lived!
Professor Harvey Rutt, University of Southampton.

☐ A BIRTH certificate bearing the name House of Windsor would be worth several millions sterling per gram.
Roger Nall, Worcester.

QUESTION: Is there a Tory equivalent of Clause 4? If

not, what would be a succinct statement of the Tories' principles and *raison d'être*?

☐ IT COULD be argued that their *raison d'être* is: 'Look after No. 1.' However, I reckon it should be: 'Look after No. 1 – and No. 1's friends.'
Les Brooksbank, Thornton, W. Yorks.

☐ SINCE 1979, the guiding principle has been: 'Government of the spiv, by the spiv and for the spiv.' What else could be expected from a party whose very name begins with a 'con'?
R. J. Wootton, Aberystwyth, Dyfed.

☐ I WOULD suggest chapter 25 verse 29 of St Matthew: 'For unto everyone that hath shall be given, and he shall have abundance: but from him that hath not shall be taken away even that which he hath.'
K. J. A. Crampton, Brockenhurst, Hants.

☐ I SUGGEST the following: 'A party of great vested interests, banded together in a formidable federation; corruption at home, aggression to cover it up abroad; the trickery of tariff juggles, the tyranny of a party machine; sentiment by the bucketful, patriotism by the imperial pint; the open hand at the public exchequer, the open door at the public house; dear food for the million, cheap labour for the millionaire.' It is taken from a speech by Winston Churchill, in Manchester 1906, when he stood as a Liberal. In the same speech he went on to say: 'We want a government that will think a little more about the toiler at the bottom of the mine and a little less about the fluctuations of the share market.'
Bob Cottingham, London N10.

☐ 'TO SECURE for ourselves by hook or by crook the full

fruits of everyone else's industry, and the fastest bucks that may be possible upon the basis of running down and flogging off the means of production, distribution and exchange, and to ensure the public are so badly educated that they keep electing us.'
Tom Freeman, Cambridge.

☐ 'EAT the poor.'
Peter Donnelly, Berkhamsted, Herts.

QUESTION: What happened to the prototype car that ran on water? Is it still a viable option? Who invented it, and is he/she still alive?

☐ IN THE early 1930s there was an experimental steam car on trial at the Sentinel Wagon Works, Shrewsbury. It was a marvellous car to drive but never commercially viable.
A. I. Pottinger, Edgbaston, Birmingham.

☐ THE idea of a spark ignition engine running on water is a common legend and was the subject of a film many years ago. After prolonged negotiations, the British Admiralty conducted a test on a small motorboat, but the 'inventor' failed to attend. The probable basis of the legend is the chemical reaction between water and calcium carbide, producing acetylene gas. Acetylene would probably burn in a suitably designed spark ignition engine, albeit badly. However, I strongly advise any interested persons not to experiment without advice: acetylene is a very unstable compound.
John Nichols, lecturer, Peterborough Regional College.

☐ IN 1897, in America, the twins Francis and Freeland Stanley introduced the first commercially successful car powered by a steam engine, the first of a series of 'Stanley

Steamers'. In 1906, on a Florida beach, the Steamer achieved a speed of 127 mph. There was at this time real uncertainty as to whether steam, electrical or internal combustion propulsion would win the day; many assumed it would be steam. But an outbreak of foot and mouth disease caused the US government to ban water troughs on the street. The troughs were essential for recharging the Steamers. By this historical accident did the internal combustion engine gain ascendancy.
Michael Glickman, London NW5.

□ YOUR enquirer probably had in mind the car that ran on water with petrol – not mixed in the tank, of course, but in the combustion chamber by a special carburettor. The idea, as I recall, was that the heat of the combustion of petrol turned the water into steam, thus adding to the energy and giving more power and/or less fuel consumption. It created a lot of interest in the 1950s and I believe it was used for a while by the Metropolitan Police.
G. M. Maclean, Market Harborough, Leics.

□ I HAVE always understood this to be a reference to cars running on hydrogen gas, derived from water. An American project, entitled the Hindenburg Project, was carrying out experiments into this some years ago, and so were BMW in Munich, but I do not know if there is any likelihood of commercial production.
Patrick Nethercot, Durham.

□ IN 1903 my grandfather W. E. Galloway went to New York and while he was there met the Stanley brothers. He was so impressed with their steam cars that he persuaded them to grant him the agency for the British Isles and the Dominions. The cars were imported direct to Newcastle upon Tyne from Boston, US, and the early models were 10 horsepower and cost £225 or £300 for special coachwork.

The American-styled body did not prove popular and soon
the imports were of the chassis only and coachbuilt bodies
were added at Gateshead. Also spares were soon made there
too. Later there was a 20 hp Gentlemen's Speedy Roadster
capable of 90 mph. My grandfather took up racing in the
north-east and won many trophies, as the steam car was
much faster than the ordinary internal combustion engine.
The steam car sold fairly well before the first world war.
About 360 were sold, but when the war came deliveries
were erratic and Stanley boilers were used in conjunction
with a pump to pump out the water from the trenches in
Europe. Steam cars were fun to drive and easy to operate
and little could go wrong apart from the need for a new
boiler, which was expensive at £50. However, they needed
nearly half an hour to warm up from cold, and even on
the 30-mile trip to Gateshead my grandfather had to stop
and refill with water. After the war it was decided not to
continue with the agency, as by that time it was difficult to
sell steam cars against the opposition and vested interests
of the internal combustion engine combines.
Michael Armstrong, St Brelade, Jersey.

□ THE only car fuelled solely by water is the 1600 cc
Volkswagen-engined 'dune buggy', invented by Stanley
Meyer in Grove City, Ohio. Water from the fuel tank is
converted into an explosive hydrogen gas mixture through
very high voltage, very low current pulses. No storage of
hydrogen is involved. The exhaust is de-energised water
vapour. The car is expected to run at up to 65 mph for 25
miles on 1 pint of water. A prototype was demonstrated
to an Ohio TV audience in 1984 and 1985. Since then
development has continued and a conversion kit for petrol
engines up to 400 hp has now been manufactured to a
pre-production standard. Further demonstrations await
clearance in accordance with the US Clean Air Act.
Anthony Griffin, Bosham, W. Sussex.

QUESTION: Why, in many European languages, is the word for the number nine so similar to the word for new?

☐ JOHN BARROW, in his book *Pi in the Sky*, discusses the origins of counting and number systems. He notes that many early cultures used a base 8 number system (possibly derived from the eight fingers, or alternatively from counting the spaces between fingers and thumbs). When the base 10 number system evolved, Barrow speculates that the number nine was called 'new' because it was the first new number in the new base system. Apparently there are about 20 examples where 'nine' and 'new' share a common etymology, including Sanskrit, Persian and Latin.
Mick Morgan, Swainsthorpe, Norfolk.

☐ WHILE I agree with Mick Morgan that a base 8 number system explains similarities between words for 'nine' and 'new' in a number of languages, I can't see why anyone would want to count the spaces between their fingers. If I were a farmer in an early 'base 8' culture, I would be unlikely to gesture 3 finger spaces across the fields to show how many chapattis I wanted for my lunch. Surely a base 8 system owes more to using the thumbs as counters, touching the four fingers.
Baljit Gill, London E8.

QUESTION: Assuming that one could construct a suitable container (and remain undiscovered), would it be cheaper to send oneself as a parcel to (e.g.) Australia than it would be to travel there by 'conventional' methods. If so, has it ever been attempted?

☐ AT CURRENT rates, the questioner could fly to Australia,

and back, five times for the cost of sending himself as a parcel.
Roger Tennant, Lutterworth, Leics.

☐ ON A track by the Velvet Underground called 'The Gift', a character called Waldo, missing his girlfriend, acquires a large cardboard box, fills it with enough food and drink, and posts himself across America to be with her. All goes well until the parcel arrives at his girlfriend's house. She has difficulty opening it so she fetches a knife, stabs at the box to break the seal, and kills him. At least he remained undiscovered!
John Tout, Backwell, Bristol.

QUESTION: What is the Club of Rome, when was it founded, what is its purpose, who are its members and how are they selected?

☐ THE Club of Rome, founded at a meeting in the city in 1968, comprises 100 leading individuals worldwide, with common concerns for the future of humanity. It is voluntary, unofficial, multi-disciplinary, with no politicians in office, and no ideological, religious, political, national or other alignment. Its purpose is non-officially to catalyse change, by focusing thinking, especially of those who govern, upon issues of growing difficulty or promise, further ahead than governments usually can. In 1991 a report by the Club emphasised 'three immediacies' requiring attention: the dispersion of armaments; environmental deterioration; and the growing poverty gaps between and within nations. Club of Rome members come from over 50 countries in five continents, with a wide mix of outlooks, religions and races.
Brian Locke, President of the British Association for the Club of Rome.

QUESTION: In Gilbert and Sullivan's opera *The Gondoliers*, the men are discovered at the opening of Act II playing various games including one called 'morra'. What is this game and how is it played?

☐ THE game is played on the fingers. The two players move simultaneously. Each shows either one or two fingers, and at the same time guesses whether the other player is showing one or two fingers. If both players guess correctly or both guess wrongly then no one loses. If only one player gets it right then he/she wins as many chips as the two players together showed fingers. The game can be expanded by agreement and played with as many fingers as the contestants have available. Though fair and simple in practice, successful play requires bluff, cunning and strategy. A detailed discussion can apparently be found in *Theory of Games and Economic Behaviour* by the mathematicians John von Neumann and Oskar Morgenstern (Princeton University Press, 1943).
Philip King, London SW9.

QUESTION: While in Moscow recently I purchased a very cheap Geiger counter. The average count both there and here was between 10 and 20. On the return flight I switched it on at 30,000 feet and was rather startled to get a reading of 298. Why? And does this have any implications for regular fliers?

☐ GEIGER counters measure radiation in terms of the number of particles encountered per second. This measurement is not directly related to the damage that the radiation might do to the human body – for that you need to use a dosemeter that gives a reading in sieverts. This measurement takes account of the type of particle, its allergy and the effect it would have on human tissue. On flights to and from Moscow I usually record a radiation dose of about 8 microsieverts, which compares with the ICRP recommended limit for the general public from industrial sources of 1,000 microsieverts per year. This is reached after about 400 hours' flying. Incidentally, on a day-long visit around the Chernobyl nuclear power station I recorded a dose of 6 microsieverts.

Steven Hall, Leigh, Lancs.

☐ EVERYONE is exposed to natural sources of radiation all the time. One of these is cosmic radiation, which originates in the sun and other galactic sources. Primary cosmic rays interact in the earth's outer atmosphere producing secondary cosmic rays, some of which penetrate the atmosphere and reach sea level. They contribute an annual radiation dose of roughly 300 microsieverts to the UK population, out of a total from all natural sources of about 2,200 microsieverts. The earth's atmosphere provides some protection against cosmic radiation. At high altitudes, such protection decreases and the cosmic ray dose rate increases dramatically – from 0.03 microsieverts/hour at sea level to 3 microsieverts/hour at 10 km altitude. Regular fliers are therefore exposed to higher radiation levels than those who remain on the earth's surface. The action of the earth's magnetic field steadily increases the cosmic ray dose from the equator towards either pole. Transpolar flights are thus more seriously affected than those over the equator. The aurora borealis (northern lights) is a visible manifestation of the interaction of cosmic rays with the atmosphere at high altitude and latitude.

Desmond MacMahon, Centre for Analytical Research in the Environment, Imperial College at Silwood Park, Ascot, Berks.

☐ THE questioner has essentially repeated the experiment

which was done when cosmic rays were discovered in 1912. Then, Victor Hess took a counter rather like a Geiger counter on a manned balloon flight, without oxygen, to 17,500 feet. He inferred the existence of cosmic radiation from the count increase which he observed.
Professor Alan Watson, Physics Department, University of Leeds.

QUESTION: What is, or was, a 'Litten Tree'? A pub of this name recently opened nearby but no one (including the pub staff) is able to answer my question.

☐ *LITTEN* is the Saxon word for a cemetery. A park in Newport, Isle of Wight, is called Church Litten. I assume, therefore, that a litten tree is the species usually found in old churchyards, the yew.
Susan Watkin, Godmanchester, Cambs.

QUESTION: When Shelley drowned in a boating accident, his wife Mary and Lord Byron burnt his body on a funeral pyre. Mary rescued his heart from the flames and kept it in a casket for the rest of her life. What happened to the heart when Mary Shelley died and where is it now?

☐ SHELLEY'S cremation, stage-managed by his friend of only six months, Trelawny, was attended by Trelawny himself; Lord Byron; Leigh Hunt, who had travelled to Italy to join Shelley and Byron in a publishing venture; and various local officers. Mary did not attend and, according to Trelawny's account, the others could hardly face it; Byron swimming off to his boat and Hunt remaining in his carriage. Trelawny observed that Shelley's heart

was not consumed in the fire and rescued it, burning his hand and risking quarantine in the process. Hunt lay claim to it from Trelawny, justifying his action to Mary, who assumed a natural right to possession in a letter: '. . . for [Hunt's love of Shelley] to make way for the claims of any other love, man's or woman's, I must have great reasons indeed brought to me . . . In *his* case above all other human beings, no ordinary appearance of rights, not even yours, can affect me.' Byron was asked to intervene but flippantly questioned Hunt's need for the heart ('He'll only . . . write sonnets on it') and it was through the efforts of Jane Williams, the Shelleys' friend, whose partner Edward had drowned with Shelley, that Hunt was eventually persuaded to part with the relic and Mary took charge of it. At Mary Shelley's death in 1851, the heart was found in her desk wrapped in a copy of 'Adonais', Shelley's self-prophesying eulogy on the death of Keats. It was kept in a shrine with other relics at Boscombe Manor, the home of Shelley's son, and finally buried in 1889 in the family vault in Bournemouth.
Abbie Mason, Cambridge.

☐ AMY WALLACE, in the second *Book of Lists*, writes: 'There is a peculiar note of irony to the whole affair. The organ that longest survives a fire is not the heart but the liver – and no one present at Shelley's funeral knew enough about anatomy to tell the difference. This theory would explain the legend that the heart was unusually large.'
David Cottis, London SW15.

☐ A MORE precise location of Shelley's heart is the graveyard of Peter's Church, Bournemouth, where it shares a resting place with the remains of other such worthies as Mary Woolstonecraft, 18th-century feminist, and Sir Dan Godfrey, founder in 1893 of the precursor of the Bournemouth Symphony Orchestra.
John Gritten, London.

☐ No ONE interested in Shelley's heart should omit to read Timothy Webb's 'Religion of the Heart' (*Keats–Shelley Review*, Autumn 1992). The reader will learn that Shelley's heart was not unusually large, but unusually small – according to Trelawny, who snatched it from the fire. It was Leigh Hunt who changed Trelawny's account probably, as Webb plausibly argued, because he could not face the idea of a Shelley with a diminished organ of benevolence. Hunt himself was well equipped to know the heart from the liver, having been much struck when young by some preserved hearts among the anatomical specimens of a Lincolnshire surgeon. So we must look for an explanation, other than anatomical confusion, for why Shelley's heart would not burn. A condition leading to progressive calcification is one possibility that has been advanced. The irony of the whole affair might well be that Shelley's heart was becoming literally, though not metaphorically, a heart of stone.
Nora Crook, Cambridge.

☐ ACCORDING to John Gritten, Mary Woolstonecraft is buried in Bournemouth. But while her body may be there, her memorial headstone is still in London's Old St Pancras churchyard, behind the station.
Paul S. Coates, University of East London.

QUESTION: Why is it commonly recommended that a bottle of red, but not white, wine should be opened and allowed to 'breathe' some time before it is drunk?

☐ *THE LAROUSSE WINES AND VINEYARDS OF FRANCE* says: 'If a wine is to be served in bottle it does not matter if it is opened three hours before it is served or at the last

moment. There can be no evaporation, and oxidisation is minimal. The quantity of oxygen that penetrates the wine after it has been uncorked is very small: it absorbs twice as much while being poured into the glass and three times as much after it has stood in the glass for 15 minutes.' Decanting, on the other hand, encourages oxidisation, which develops the bouquet – but only if the wine's structure can withstand exposure to air. *Larousse* recommends that a very old wine should be opened at the last moment and should not be decanted.
David Barker, Birmingham.

QUESTION: Whenever I have written to a government department, questioning a decision they have made, I get fobbed off with a bland reply. When I have written back asking what is the basis for the answers, I hear nothing. Do I have a right to a reply?

□ You could make an application to the High Court for a judicial review of your dispute – but this is an expensive and time-consuming activity (and unbearably dull). You could use clause 5 of the Government's insipid *Code of Practice on Access to Government Information* (available by telephoning 0345-223242), which requires responses to be sent within 20 working days from the date of receipt. The code's remedy, if a department fails to supply information within this target period, is for you to refer the matter to the Parliamentary Commissioner for Administration (the Ombudsman) via your MP. I have found an almost foolproof way of eliciting information from most government departments and agencies. Firstly, my headed notepaper reads: 'Author and Journalist'. Anyone can call themselves an author, even if their only literary claim is to have penned letters of complaint to government departments. Secondly, if a reply to your

initial request (which should always be polite, lucid and to the point) is not forthcoming within, say, 14 days, then a copy of the original should be sent with a reminder. One can add a suitable caveat along the lines: 'I reserve the right to disclose the content of this correspondence to representatives of the media if this will help to facilitate a public debate on the subject.' If you really want to upset your enemy, you should send a copy to your MP – and mention this in the letter. Forget the Ombudsman; a letter of complaint sent to an MP will usually be channelled directly to the appropriate minister (even if you are represented by the most spineless political toady) and goes straight to the top of the pile. Finally, learn how to write and produce a simple press release. Using these simple skills one can launch a mini lobbying campaign for less than the price of a pint!
David Northmore, London N10.

☐ IT IS obvious from David Northmore's faith in 'spineless political toady' MPs, that he doesn't live where I do. When enquiring about government plans for education, Eric Forth of the Department for Education sent me a copy of the white paper *Choice and Diversity*. He invited me to join the consultation process by sending my comments and questions about it through my MP, an invitation endorsed by that same MP. I did so, upon which my MP, after acknowledging that I was an intelligent and articulate person, refused to pass them on as he had promised. His argument was that my comments were hypothetical (as indeed were the policies in the white paper until he voted them into law), and that he preferred to spend his time dealing with constituents who had real problems. *My* Conservative MP opted out of the democratic consultation process which, of course, raises the questions as to whose views he did pass on to education ministers?
Eileen Hathaway, Swanage, Dorset.

□ WHILST I agree with David Northmore that various devices can be used to irritate government departments, the real reason for the bland reply is that the person does not know the answer to the question. This is because he or she works in a customer services department whose mission is to meet some bogus Citizen's Charter target. This requires a response within 'x' working days. The content of the letter is irrelevant. Much better to fob people off on time than take the trouble to give them a proper reply. Anyway, in 90 per cent of the cases the answer is the same: the quality of service has been diminished as a result of government spending cuts or a management reorganisation.
R. M. Hawkes, London N20.

□ IF I fail to get a reasonably quick reply from a business or government organisation, I send a full frontal picture postcard of the Cerne Abbas Giant to the managing director or chief executive. Everyone in the firm sees and reads it before the chief gets it, and a reply usually arrives by return of post.
Richard Harvey, Salisbury, Wilts.

□ I WROTE to Tony Blair raising a number of questions about his irrational attack on Clause 4. From an underling I received a bland reply. Is this preparation for government?
Councillor Douglas McCarrick, Moseley, Birmingham.

QUESTION: My mother taught me that when making tea I should always warm the pot. Does this actually do any good, and if so what? Is it different if you are using tea bags?

□ THE hotter the water remains after pouring on to the

leaves, the more quickly the tea will infuse and the fresher it will taste. For most teas, four or five minutes is ideal. If boiling water is poured into a cold pot its temperature is at once lowered, resulting in a loss either of strength or of freshness. This applies equally to teabags if a pot is used.
Alex Barlow, Ilford, Essex.

☐ A POINT Alex Barlow omitted to mention is the heat capacity of the vessel in which the tea is being brewed. A large thick china pot will abstract more heat from the boiling water than a small thin metal one. Thus it is more important to warm the former.
R. Pearce, Helston, Cornwall.

☐ TO MAKE a good pot of black tea, water should be poured on to the leaves at a temperature of 95–98°C (green teas require a temperature of 70°C). The boiling water releases three important chemicals in the fresh tea leaf – caffeine, essential oils and polyphenols. The oils are an important constituent of the tea's aroma, while polyphenols give it pungency, colour and flavour.
Jane Pettigrew, editor, Tea International, *London EC4.*

QUESTION: When did Gothic architecture become so called (the Goths and Vandals destroyed Rome, so 'Gothic' implies 'anti-Classical' in architectural terms)? Was it a term of abuse by Renaissance architects?

☐ RENAISSANCE architects did not, in general, care much for Gothic architecture with its buildings' lack of symmetry, piecemeal alterations and extensions, and messy exteriors – pinnacles, flying buttresses and knobby towers. All this conflicted with the refinements of the rediscovered Classical ideals. Giorgio Vasari (1511–74), an Italian Renaissance artist, therefore equated medieval architecture with the barbarism of the ancient Goths and Vandals, coining the term 'Gothic', a term of derision as your questioner suggests. But Sir Christopher Wren did appreciate the achievements of his predecessors, particularly at Salisbury; however, he still felt it prudent to conceal his flying buttresses from view behind screens at St Paul's.

Tim McCormick, Malvern, Worcs.

QUESTION: Is it true the average height of Britons has increased by a foot or more over the last few centuries? Is this phenomenon caused by improved diet? When will we stop growing?

☐ IN 1873, the medical officer and the natural science master at Marlborough College measured the height of 500 or so of the pupils. At sixteen and a half years the average height of the boys was 65.5 inches. When a comparable sample was measured 80 years later, the average was 69.6 inches – equivalent to a gain of half an inch a decade. James Tanner (in *Foetus into Man*, 1978) makes the point that such trends in children's height are at least partially accountable in terms of earlier maturity. The so-called secular trend at completion of stature in adulthood is in the region of 4 inches in a hundred years. He did not detect a slowing-down in the trend. Although improved standards of nutrition are cited as one possible cause, Tanner also invokes a genetic explanation, which in turn hangs on the increased incidence of marriages and procreation outside the village community. He notes that a key factor in the growth of this 'outbreeding' was the introduction of the bicycle.

Peter Barnes, Milton Keynes.

☐ THE study of skeletons from archaeological excavations has shown that the average height of the population within the British Isles (and elsewhere) has varied over time, and there is no doubt that the single most important influence is that of diet. In this present era of food surpluses and balanced diets in Europe, most people will grow to their full genetic potential (unless other factors such as smoking or ill health intervene). But earlier generations were acutely prone to the fluctuations of harvests, poverty and starvation – unless they were members of privileged groups. Skeletons of wealthy lay-people found in excavations I directed at Norton Priory in Cheshire showed their height to be little different in range to that of the present-day population. The peasant population of the same era tended not to grow as tall, and would usually die much younger.

Dr Patrick Greene, Director, Museum of Science and Industry in Manchester.

☐ AVERAGE young male height around 1750 was about 160 cm (63 inches) and in 1980 it was 176 cm (69.3 inches); there is no evidence of growth as large as another 6 inches in earlier centuries. The answer is complex because there has always been significant variation in height between social classes, although the inequality has narrowed over time; it therefore matters whom you measure. The average height of public school boys has risen less than that of working-class children. This fact helps to answer the second question: the primary cause of growth is increased income, which means that people can eat more, although changes in disease and pollution can have effects. But it also means that the increased income inequality since 1979 may be affecting average heights and variation between classes. We do not know when we will stop growing; in Britain we still have a long way to go to catch up with richer nations such as

the Netherlands, where young males average over 180 cm (71 inches).
Roderick Floud (co-author of Height, Health and History, *CUP), London Guildhall University.*

□ LET'S assume that there have been humans or human-like beings for some 2 million years or, say, 100,000 generations. If their average height increased each generation by a mere one-thousandth of an inch, we should now be 8 feet 4 inches taller than our remote ancestors. It seems, therefore, that there are powerful influences restricting humans to a fairly narrow variation in height, even over long periods of time.
Louis Judson, Penrith, Cumbria.

QUESTION: What happens to the royal family's old clothes?

□ I DON'T know about the old clothes, but the emperor's new suit is hanging in my wardrobe.
Ian McMahon, Barrhead, Glasgow.

QUESTION: In one of the 'soaps' the inhabitants of a small village have decided to change its name. In real life would governmental or local authority permission be required, and who would pay for the necessary changes to maps, documents and road signs, etc.?

□ WHILE working for the Ordnance Survey on the postwar resurvey of Great Britain, I became involved in several attempts by local residents to change village names. In the 19th century, before today's local authority infrastructure, evidence of rural names that were to be used on OS mapping was collected from landowners, justices of the peace, clergymen and other local worthies. On the last survey this was still the practice, but more weight was given to local authority opinion. In the early 1980s I discovered strong local opinion to change the name of Blackburn, a small village about 5 miles north of Aberdeen, to Kinellar, an older and more Scottish-sounding name. Despite a petition and lobbying of the local council, the name remained as Blackburn, and I assume mail is still being misdirected to Lancashire. A more recent debate focused on Driffield – or is it Great Driffield? There was concern in the town that business was suffering because of the difficulty of finding the name in geographic indexes under 'D'. I believe 'Driffield' has been officially adopted and will appear on all OS mapping.

Peter J. Adams, Harrogate, N. Yorks.

QUESTION: It is supposedly possible to 'prove' scientifically that a bumble bee is incapable of flying. What is the basis of this proof and where does it fall down?

☐ SIMPLE calculations involving the mass of a bee, and the lift it can achieve by the simple flapping of its wings, show that it 'cannot fly'. To non-scientists the contradiction between theory and observation is a source of considerable mirth; however, to a scientist it indicates that bees may be doing something rather interesting and are therefore worth closer study. This is confirmed by high-speed photography. A bee does not flap its wings like a bird; rather, after the down stroke, a bee's wing rotates forwards about the axis of its leading edge. On the return stroke the leading edge sweeps backwards, with the rest of the wing below it, before rising back to its original position. In effect the bee's remarkably agile wing movements provided lift on both down and

up strokes, in contrast to a bird's flapping motion.
Dr K. Sheach, Harlow, Essex.

☐ THE technical problem in the matter of the bumble bee
is that the bee's wing muscles cannot contract and relax fast
enough to account for the rate of the bumble bee's wing beat.
The bee gets over this problem by dint of having its wing
roots embedded in a special block of material that vibrates
when 'twitched' by a muscle – rather like a stretched elastic
band does when we ping it. The bee's wings, embedded in
the block, vibrate in time with the block and the bee only
needs to keep 'pinging' it to keep itself flying.
W. A. Spring, Frankfurt am Main.

**QUESTION: If one accepts 25 December as the birthday
of Jesus, were the remaining six days of the year in 1 BC
or AD 1?**

☐ WHEN Dionysius Exiguus invented the Christian era,
in its sixth century, he calculated that the Conception had
occurred on 25 March and the Nativity on 25 December
of what he called Anno Domini (in the year of the Lord)
1. So not only the last six days but also the first 328 days
of the year in which Jesus was believed to have been born
were all in AD 1.
Nicolas Walter, London N1.

☐ NEITHER: the whole year was 0, BC or AD as you prefer.
The first (full) year 'before Christ' had ended the previous
31 December; the first (full) 'year of the Lord' did not
begin until the following 1 January.
James Babbage, Cheltenham, Glos.

☐ DIONYSIUS not only didn't know the date, he also got the
year wrong. Herod, the great villain of the Nativity story,

died in 4 BC and the correct answer must be that these six days were in neither 1 BC nor AD 1 but in something about 6 BC! Incidentally, if 6 BC really was the year of Jesus's birth and so the true first year of the Christian era, 2,000 years was completed on 31 December 1994.
William Somerville, London.

□ BC/AD is now obsolete and has been replaced by BCE/CE (before common era/common era). So both the period before and after 25 December in the year attributed to Christ's birth would be 1 CE.
P. R. Rowland, Dulwich, London SE24.

□ Contrary to James Babbage's suggestion, a zero cannot refer to a period of time any more than to a unit of scale on a chart or a length marked out on a ruler. In space or time, it can refer only to a point – such as the point represented by the first marking on the ruler, or midnight on 31 December, 1 BC. The first decade of the Christian, or common, era began at the point 0 and was completed at the end of the 10th year; similarly, the second millennium will be completed at the end of the 2,000th year. This would be obvious were it not for the accident that in English, unlike some other languages, a year is designated by a cardinal rather than an ordinal number.
Paul Fletcher, Glasgow.

□ The situation is further confused by the fact that Quirinius, said by Luke to be governor of Syria at the time of the census, was not in fact around until about AD 10, some years after the death of Herod, while the only recorded census in the area took place in AD 6. These problems notwithstanding, estimates for Jesus' birth vary between 11–4 BC; 7 BC seems to be about best guess.
Gavin Saxton, Glenrothes, Fife.

QUESTION: In Europe, Santa Claus wears a long red cloak; in America, he sports a belted jacket, with trousers tucked into black boots. When and why did this divergence occur?

☐ THE American Santa was largely the invention of the illustrator Thomas Nast, who produced several of the red-jacket, belt and boots version of St Claus as accompaniment to the 1863 imprint of Clement Clarke's 1822 poem 'A Visit from St Nicholas'. One of the few things to have disappeared since Nast's trail-blazing is Santa's long clay pipe. The dinky belt and boots image was given added fizz in the 1930s when Coca-Cola coerced Santa into their advertising campaign in full company colours. The Euro-model, on the other hand, derives from Father Christmas, a different – and older – character altogether. He was a feature of medieval mumming plays, and owed much to festive gods such as Woden and Bacchus. The Father Christmas/Santa distinction was still clear last century, before the Americans had conquered world culture. FC was sometimes depicted wearing crowns of holly or carrying a cross. He occasionally wore colours other than red too. Those interested should seek out Mary Baker's *Who is Father Christmas?* or *Maypoles, Martyres and Mayhem* by Quentin Cooper and Paul Sullivan (Bloomsbury).
Paul Sullivan, Odiham, Hants.

☐ WHEN I was a child in Poland, Christmas presents were brought not by the tubby, jolly Santa whom my children know, but by a stately bishop, complete with robe, mitre and staff. He was a dignified and rather awesome figure, who before giving out presents asked you whether you had been good and often required a little poem or prayer to be recited first. He was called Saint Nicholas. During the 1950s the Communists desperately tried to oust the saintly

bishop and substitute him with a more proletarian figure of Grandpa Frost. They failed, but over the years Saint Nicholas gradually lost his dignity and somehow evolved into the red-cloaked, gnome-like creature we know today. Only the name remained.
Ania Plank, Amersham, Bucks.

QUESTION: If Christ returned, how likely is it that he would become a Christian?

☐ IT IS certain that he would continue to propagate the ethic he left first time round; but it is unlikely he would identify himself with the mythology, ritual and dogma in which this ethic has become wrapped in the last 2,000 years.
Gordon Rudlin, Stonesfield, Witney, Oxon.

☐ IF WE accept the Nicene Creed as the formal statement of Christian belief or dogma, then we should ask ourselves how it would have been viewed by a Galilean rabbi of the Second Temple Period – not that this would have been possible, because some of the points of faith in the creed were not yet invented. However, our 1st-century rabbi would have probably accepted about one-third of it, regarded about another third as blasphemous, and would have found the remaining third incomprehensible. Therefore the man Jesus could not have been a Christian. The Christ is a very different being, an incarnate god. The title Christos – 'the anointed one' – and the term 'Christian' were applied after the death of Jesus, and owe much more to Greece than to Israel.
Philip D. Whitehead, Penarth, S. Glamorgan.

☐ CHRIST would be appalled by the gross injustices and stupidities of the present human society, and by the wide

extent of cruelty, lust for power, intolerance, selfishness and greed. He would ask us: 'Why are you crucifying me again?', and why our over-commercialised capitalist world order is worshipping Mammon instead of God. At the same time, He would strongly support and encourage the humanitarian initiatives and projects being carried out by so many people of goodwill around the world – often under very difficult conditions and against tremendous opposition. Instead of joining any particular religion or political party, He would reaffirm the fundamental ethical and spiritual truths behind *all* the great religions, and present a unified altruistic practical philosophy for our times. As in His previous incarnation, He would live by setting a good example for all of us, by accomplishing His ministry of healing, and by increasing our awareness.
Alan J. Mayne, Downhead Park, Milton Keynes.

☐ VERY soon, I believe, your readers and the world will know the answer. For 20 years, I have sought, by world-wide lectures, books, *Share International Magazine* (as editor) and innumerable TV and radio interviews, to make known the imminence of His return and, since 19 July 1977, the *fact* of His presence in the Asian community of London. He has come, as He predicted through Jesus, 'like a thief in the night, in such an hour as you think not', and not from 'heaven' but from His ancient spiritual retreat in the Himalayas; from where, as the Embodiment of the Christ Principle or Consciousness, His mind 'overshadowed' that of Jesus from the Baptism to the Crucifixion. This time, He has come Himself as the leader of a large group of spiritually enlightened men, including Jesus. He is not a religious teacher *per se*, but an educator in the broadest sense, showing the need for *spiritual*, political, economic and social structures if we are to survive. He has not come to found a new religion nor to create followers, but to teach humanity 'the Art of Self or God, Realisation'. Awaited

by Christians as the Christ, by Jews as the Messiah, by
Moslems as the Imam Mahdi, by Hindus as Krishna and by
Buddhists under His personal name as *Maitreya* Buddha,
He is the World Teacher for all groups – religious and
non-religious alike.
Benjamin Creme, London NW5.

**QUESTION: The Archbishop of Canterbury bears the
title Primate of All England. The Archbishop of York
bears that of Primate of England. Why this apparent
distinction without a difference?**

☐ WHEN St Augustine arrived in this country in 597, he
was charged with organising England into two provinces
with Archbishops of London and York. Canterbury took
the place of London immediately. The struggle for precedence was finally settled by Pope Innocent VI who
gave the Archbishop of Canterbury the title of Primate
of All England, the Archbishop of York to be known as
the Primate of England (source: *The Oxford Dictionary
of the Christian Church*).
Revd Michael Westney, Burnham, Slough, Berks.

**QUESTION: How automatic is the automatic pilot on
an aeroplane? And can we do away with human pilots
altogether?**

☐ MAJOR advances are being made with the complexity
of computer technology in the civil aviation industry. It is
now confidently predicted that the flight-deck crew of large
airliners will soon comprise a single pilot, accompanied by
a dog. The primary task of the pilot will be to feed the
dog. The role of the dog will be to bite the pilot if he or
she attempts to touch anything.
M. J. Ingham, Nettleham, Lincoln.

☐ THE term Autopilot is rather misleading, being the trade name for the German control system used in the Graf-Zeppelin L7127 in 1927. Aircraft Flight Control Systems are essential for the safe operation of modern civilian and military aircraft and contribute to an aircraft's stability. No aircraft is 'really' stable in flight, and continuous adjustments have to be made in order to maintain straight and level flight. If a pilot is on a long-haul journey, the continuous manipulation of rudder and flaps (especially in windy conditions) would be exhausting. The AFCSs are designed to make life easier. As for doing away with human pilots altogether, unless an electronic system can be made to anticipate all possible eventualities and to act appropriately then we shall have to stick with humanity. If an airline ever proposes to introduce self-flying pilot-free aircraft then remember – it's your life!
Gregory Slaughter, York.

QUESTION: I have been told that there are only three villages in England where all the men called up for the first world war returned home safely. They are known as 'The Thankful Three'. One is Upper Slaughter. What are the other two?

☐ ARTHUR MEE'S *The King's England – Somerset* claims that there are 31 'Thankful villages' in England, seven of which are in Somerset – Alsholt, Chelwood, Rodney Stoke, Stocklinch, Stanton Prior, Tellisford and Woolley.
K. J. Treanor, Bridgwater, Somerset.

QUESTION: Has anyone ever changed their voting

intention as a result of watching a party political broadcast?

☐ YES. As an enthusiastic and naïve 18-year-old I witnessed my first PPB. Result? I decided not to vote.
James Timothy, Fife.

☐ WINSTON CHURCHILL made a party political speech just before the election, after world war two. I had been an admirer of Churchill throughout the war. After listening to the speech, detailing the catastrophe of a possible Labour victory, I performed two *volte-faces*. I voted Labour and joined the Labour Party.
Cliff Preston, Stockport, Cheshire.

QUESTION: Who is the world's most popular singer, as measured by number of recordings sold? I've been told it's Mohammad Rafi.

☐ I BELIEVE the answer is Julio Iglesias, who has allegedly sold more records in more languages than any other musical artiste in the history of recorded music. As long ago as 1983 he was the first ever recipient of a Diamond Disc for topping 100 million sales world-wide. Today he has almost doubled that achievement. He has recorded 70 albums in six languages which have consistently topped charts in 90 countries over 25 years. His career trophies are said to include over 1,000 gold and 350 platinum discs.
Tim Wapshott, London E2.

QUESTION: What is the origin of the expression 'raining cats and dogs'? I note that Thomas de Quincey used it in *Confessions of an Opium Eater*, written about 1820.

☐ IN THE pre-industrial city, when there was no adequate drainage, but a large population of stray animals, it was not unusual to find drowned cats and dogs in the streets after a violent rainstorm. Hence, 'it's been raining cats and dogs'.
Patrick Hennessy, Paris.

☐ YOU might be interested in the German (Austrian) equivalent phrase: 'It's raining cobblers' apprentices.'
Eric Sanders, London W12.

☐ IN AFRIKAANS, the equivalent expression is '*dit reent oumeide met knopkieries*,' which literally means 'it's raining grandmothers with knobkerries.'
Robert J. Newman, Croydon, Surrey.

☐ WHILST not knowing the origin, I am certain it pre-dates the expression 'hailing taxis'.
D. A. Dyer, Mayland, Chelmsford, Essex.

☐ IN NORTH Wales the expression is '*bwrw hen wragedd a ffyn*' – 'raining old women and sticks'; in South Wales it is '*eyllyll a ffyre*' – 'knives and forks'.
R. P. W. Lewis, Earley, Reading.

QUESTION: A packet of cigarettes carries the government health warning: 'Smoking kills.' If the same government directly profits from the sale of the cigarettes (through taxation), what is to stop them being successfully prosecuted as an accessory to murder?

☐ AS WE all have a choice as to whether to smoke or not, neither the Government nor the tobacco companies could be said to be guilty of murder, only of aiding suicide. And in the case of death or illness caused by

passive smoking, it is almost impossible to prove that passive smoking was the cause or major cause of, for example, asthma. Such a disease may also have been caused by, or aggravated by, pollution. Also, if an illness was caused by passive smoking, then it could be said to be the smokers, rather than the Government, who should be prosecuted. A successful prosecution against a tobacco company for the diseases caused by passive smoking was brought in America. However, the circumstances were that the prosecutor's lungs were injured in his childhood due to his parents' smoking. This occurred prior to the tobacco companies putting health warnings on their cigarette packets. Finally, the Government and the tobacco companies have far more money than most individuals, and they also have a vested interest in stopping any individual from setting such a dangerous precedent.
Amy Binns, Edinburgh.

☐ Not murder, I'm afraid, but surely 'living off immoral earnings'. *Et tu, Guardian*, with your full-page paid ads for the lethal things!
Roger Franklin, Stroud, Glos.

QUESTION: Is it true that we use only 10 per cent of our brain? If so, what is the proof and why have we evolved a 90 per cent redundant brain?

☐ The brain, the rest of the nervous system and the body itself form an integrated system, much of which functions at the optimum level all the time. So what would it mean to claim that the parts of the brain concerned with sight, smell or touch were only working at 10 per cent of some theoretical capacity? Of course the different cognitive functions such as memory, learning or problem-solving can be improved by practise and training; but not everyone

is able to do so to the same extent (or even feels the need
to do so), and there is no evidence to suggest this kind of
improved performance involves hitherto 'quiet' areas of
the brain. In humans, the brain is the most metabolically
expensive organ, taking about 20 per cent of the available
oxygen and energy – so evolution will have given us the
largest brain we can efficiently maintain. The figure of 10
per cent which always seems to be quoted is a classic case
of using numbers plucked out of nowhere to give spurious
respectability to a statement for which there is no other
supporting evidence.
Michael Hutton, Camberwell, London SE5.

**QUESTION: Why do stage and comic drunks always
sing: 'There's an old mill by the stream, Nellie
Dean . . .'?**

☐ IN THE United States, drunks traditionally sing 'Come
to me, my melancholy baby.' The songs share two features
which make them suitable for portraying inebriation; a
tone of self-pitying nostalgia, and a first line that ends
with long vowel sounds, giving the singer an opportunity
to stretch out the final notes with head thrown back, arms
spread wide, and bottle in hand.
David Cottis, Putney, London.

**QUESTION: If a poisonous snake accidentally bites
itself, does it die?**

☐ THE hunting strategies of front-fanged snakes (rattle-
snakes, cobras, etc.) make this highly unlikely. But
during inter-male fighting among some species it is
possible that, if one protagonist injects a full load of
venom, the other may die. More interestingly, some snake

species which (although non-venomous themselves) prey on other, potently toxic snakes, have sufficient immunity to survive being bitten.
Ray Cimino, wildlife consultant, Dublin.

QUESTION: Can anyone tell me when and how the differences between US and UK spelling began?

☐ UNLIKE other European languages, e.g. French or German, no central or Royal authority was set up in England to formalise or standardise language usage, oral or written (the King's English was that accent of the Court). In spelling, various conventions were adopted depending on whether there were Anglo-Saxon, French, Greek or Latin roots or indeed any admixture. For a generally accepted spelling of particular words to gain adoption, the development of an independent dictionary regarded as authoritative had to arrive. The American publisher Webster managed to gain an almost complete dominance of the US market during the 19th century and became their authoritative source. The UK market was more fractured and it was not until publication in the late 19th/early 20th century of Murray/Oxford English dictionaries – which provided an exhaustive account of the history of the language – that 'English spelling' had an exemplar authority.
Tony Sharp, Southwark, London SE1.

QUESTION: What happened to Freddie Phillips who wrote the music to *Camberwick Green*, *Trumpton* and *Chigley*? Has he written anything else?

☐ THANKS to the questioner for his interest. I am still on the raft at the age of 75! I have written much more

music besides the above scores. My other television work includes: *Man in the Suitcase* (serial), *The Hunchback of Notre Dame* (serial), *The Rose Tattoo* (Play of the Week), *Men of Our Time – Gandhi*. In theatre: *The Rose Tattoo* (production by Sam Wanamaker), *Orpheus Descending* (production by Tony Richardson at the Royal Court Theatre).
Freddie Phillips, West Ewell, Surrey.

QUESTION: My hearing being slightly impaired, I often use Teletext subtitles when watching television. But when playing back from a video recording Teletext is completely garbled. Why is this? Is there any solution?

☐ TV PICTURES are made up from 625 horizontal lines, transmitted 25 times a second. About 40 of these are off the top of the screen, and not shown on a normally adjusted TV set. On some of these lines, the Teletext information is broadcast as dots. The text of the page can contain codes that change the colour or a switch to 'graphics' mode. In this mode, each letter is redisplayed as a blocky graphic. The colour codes occupy a 'space' on the page. This is why Teletext pages look very distinctive. Codes can also make the text superimpose over a television picture for subtitles and newsflashes. VHS video recorders are not designed to record the whole picture that is transmitted, as the tape is not capable of holding all the information. This is why a video-cassette picture is inferior to that of a well-tuned television picture. Where a video does record the off-the-screen lines, it only makes an approximate copy of the Teletext information. So when the video is replayed the garbled Teletext data cannot be interpreted by the small Teletext computer in the television set.
Brian N. Butterworth, BT Broadcast Services.

☐ THE solution is either a special adaptor or preferably a Teletext VCR. There are a few of these on the market but their numbers are decreasing partly due to the prevalence of VideoPlus (and lack of consumer pressure). Super-VHS machines are also an (exclusive) option. If the questioner would like a list of suitable VCRs, he is welcome to write to me – my address is on BBC2 Ceefax, page 710.
Chas Donaldson, Editor of Read Hear *and BBC subtitler, Glasgow.*

☐ BRIAN BUTTERWORTH gives an incorrect explanation of the problem. A VHS machine does record the whole picture. There is some tearing at the bottom of the picture when the recorder switches from one head to the other, but this has nothing to do with the Teletext which is recorded above the top of the picture. The garbled text is produced because the VHS system records the minimum bandwidth necessary for watchable pictures and this is insufficient for Teletext data which contains significantly higher frequencies. The effect is precisely the same as filtering out all the higher frequencies from speech – when the 'woolly sock' effect becomes too severe the results are unintelligible. S-VHS and other formats that produce a sharper picture, one with a greater content of high frequencies, can record Teletext quite reliably.
Chris Woolf, Liskeard, Cornwall.

☐ THERE are 14 million people in the UK who use subtitles. Hopefully the VCR manufacturers will realise that there is a large market for VCRs which can record subtitles, especially with the growth of the 'grey market', and include this feature in future models.
Steve Stratton, Principal Technical Awareness Officer, Royal National Institute for Deaf People (RNID), London WC1.

☐ I HAVE found that recording programmes from cable television will preserve all the on-screen text uncorrupted – without the need for a special video recorder or adaptor. *David A. Smith, Ealing, London W5.*

QUESTION: Who was Hobson and what was the choice he had to make?

☐ THOMAS HOBSON (1545–1631) was a well-known Cambridge figure. As the 'University Carrier' he plied his trade for many years, hiring out horses for long distance travel. The Bull Inn in Bishopsgate was his stopping-place in London. According to Milton, who wrote two epitaphs to commemorate Hobson's death, his business appears to have failed when he was 'forbidden to travel to London by reason of the plague' and he fell ill and died during this involuntary 'vacancy'. The expression 'Hobson's choice' originated in his practice of hiring out hackney horses in strict rotation, making each customer take the horse which stood nearest the stable door (Steele: *Spectator* 509; 14 October 1712).
Kayode Robbin-Coker, Southwark Street, London SE1.

QUESTION: What is the evolutionary benefit to parrots of being able to talk?

☐ WHEN, as often occurs, a parrot gets sick, it can describe its exact symptoms to the vet. This of course increases its chances of survival.
D. L. Foster, Stanks, Leeds.

☐ BENEFITS include the increased likelihood of human interest, bringing food and shelter. However, the plight of the performing parrot can be likened to that of the

struggling actor: being pigeon-holed into limited roles, which do not allow one to spread one's wings, and which are rewarded with peanuts and a poor standard of living.
Simon Stoker, Farnham, Surrey.

☐ IT'S just another myna miracle.
Peter Barnes, Simpson, Bucks.

QUESTION: How did people refer to the colour orange before the discovery of the fruit?

☐ THERE are several possibilities. Yellow, for instance, has had a broader range than now (cf. *jaune* in French). 'Gold' and 'amber' are used as colours before the late 16th-century arrival of 'orange': for instance, from the *Secretis secretorum* of the early 15th century: 'Whos colour ys gold, lyke that ys meen bytwen reed and yalwe.' Chaucer describes Chaunticleer: 'His colour was between yellow and red.' But the most common term was probably 'tawny'. Holland's Pliny of 1601 has 'without forth of a light tawny or yellowish-red'. The definitive answer is probably from heraldic terms, as the field is an ancient one that relies on greater accuracy in colour definitions than we vulgarians require. So Leigh's *Armorie* of 1562: 'Now to the sixth coloure, whiche we calle Tawney, and is blazed by thys woorde, Tenne . . . it is made of two bright colours which is redde and yellowe.'
Jonny Morris, Reading.

☐ THE colour we now call 'orange' was regarded as 'yellow'. The development of dyes allowed shade variations of 'ochre' and the darker variation is still known as 'burnt ochre', the brighter as 'yellow ochre'. The original name for the fruit was 'a norange', and through verbal elision became 'an orange'. It was described as of yellow colour. The brighter shade of burnt ochre became informally the name of the fruit when the citrus became a regular household object and the dye colours stabilised around standards. In Spanish, where oranges originated in Europe, the fruit is called *naranja* and its colour there is amarillo, i.e. yellow.

Tony Sharp, Southwark, London SE1.

☐ YOUR correspondents' replies about the colour orange having formerly been regarded as a category of the colour yellow need qualifying. It could also be seen as a category of the colour red. John Parkinson, in his *Paradisus Terrestris* (1629), describes the 'Orange tree' as having fruit which 'are (as all men know) red on the outside, some more pale than others, and some kinds of a deeper yellowish red.'

Dr Brent Elliott, Royal Horticultural Society, London SW1.

☐ IN ROGER BACON'S scale of 21 colours published in the 13th century, the term 'puniceus' was used to refer to the colour between yellow/red and red/gold and was presumably the modern orange. This may be connected with Punic wax, a yellowish substance used instead of oil by painters in ancient Greece.

Dennis Griffiths, Southampton.

☐ IF ROGER BACON used the word 'puniceus' to refer to the colour between yellow and red, I imagine it would mean 'pomegranate-like'. *Punica* is the Latin name of that fruit which is orange-ish in colour.

Eileen Bernard, St Martin's, Oswestry, Shropshire.

QUESTION: Are the graves used in films specially dug, or are they just waiting to be filled?

☐ 'FILLED' graves are almost always real ones. Care is taken to get permission from relatives where names, etc., on headstones may be readable on camera. 'Unfilled', i.e. open, graves are always specially dug – with permission from the graveyard authorities – to the specifications of the film-script.

Don Henderson, Legionknight Film & TV Production Company, Stratford-upon-Avon, Warks.

QUESTION: What is the text of the chorus of grunting featured in Ennio Morricone's film score *The Good, the Bad and the Ugly*?

☐ AMONG many theories the favourite is that it is designer gibberish which will seem strangely familiar yet not quite comprehensible to audiences of different nationalities. There are precedents for this technique, most notably in Prokofiev's score for Eisenstein's *Alexander Nevsky*, in which nonsensical, dog-Latin chanting accompanies the invading Teutonic crusaders. Morricone himself used a similar device in parts of his score for *The Mission*.

Les Jepson, Worksop, Notts.

QUESTION: In Portugal last year, I watched as a shepherd moved a large flock of sheep from a field on one side of the road to a field on the other side simply by whistling instructions to the sheep. At sheep-dog trials in this country, are we being had?

☐ POSSIBLY. On the other hand British sheep may have something Portuguese sheep haven't. Watch *One Man and His Dog* to observe the sheep lurking in the undergrowth, waiting for a dim dog to catch up with them; or see them wind up shepherd and dog by refusing to enter the pen. Or it may be the Portuguese sheep simply believe that the grass is greener on the other side of the hedge.

R. A. Leeson, Broxbourne, Herts.

☐ FLOCKS that are worked with dogs are controlled by fear – the dog is a natural predator of sheep. So the shepherd uses his or her authority to curb the dog's instinct to attack the sheep. I choose to manage my flock of 100 ewes without a dog, and I find this rewarding because it makes for a closer relationship with my sheep. They tend to run towards people rather than away. Normally, the sheepdog responds to whistled commands and manoeuvres the sheep. I have cut out the middleman and just call up the sheep with whistles.

Mrs G. D. Wolstenholme, Llandeilo, Dyfed.

QUESTION: Why is the road surface on French autoroutes and other main roads much smoother and of finer composition than equivalents in Britain?

☐ FRENCH road-building contractors are encouraged to innovate, whereas their British counterparts are stuck with Department of Transport specifications which refuse to recognise that new techniques can offer advantages. The best example of this is the use of a paving material called porous asphalt. This allows water to drain through a series of interconnecting voids, rather than sit on top of the road. This greatly increases safety by reducing the risk of aquaplaning, and improves visibility by reducing spray. A spin-off benefit of porous asphalt is that it reduces road noise by about half – the voids serve to deaden the noise which would otherwise be reflected. This in turn improves comfort and reduces driver fatigue – another safety advantage. These qualities have made porous asphalt very popular in many European countries – in Austria it is called 'political asphalt' because of its reduction of environmental noise. A stretch of the A38 Burton-upon-Trent bypass was surfaced using the material over 10 years ago, and is still performing well; but the DoT remains extremely conservative. One reason cited is that the material is slightly more expensive than conventional asphalt, but numerous studies have shown that the savings in accidents more than make up for this. The company which is building the Birmingham Expressway (the first privately owned toll road in Britain for 200 years) has indicated that it might use the material – so that drivers will get a premium service in return for paying the toll. Paradoxically, porous asphalt is a British invention, developed in the 1950s to improve friction on airfields.

Russ Swan, Editor, World Highways, *Nottingham.*

☐ RUSS SWAN rightly points out that the Government has been extremely reluctant to sponsor improved highway standards, the key example being the quiet road surface, porous asphalt. The efforts of myself and others to have the porous asphalt surface laid on the section of the A34 that skirts East Ilsley, near Newbury, came to no avail. Villagers now have to put up with incessant road noise, made more intolerable by the fact that it was avoidable. Work on the A34 Newbury bypass is due to commence during the winter. There is again a glaring need for the new road to feature porous asphalt. The Government could at least show that it is capable of understanding public fears. A quiet road surface on the bypass would be a good start.

David Rendel MP, London SW1.

☐ THE surface of our main roads is made deliberately rough to provide more grip between the tyre and road surface when travelling at higher speeds. In the wet this

roughness plays an important role by preventing water building up in front of the tyre, which could otherwise cause aquaplaning and loss of control. As a result we have one of the lowest levels of people killed on our roads per head of population both in Europe and further afield.
Nigel Organ, Head of Road Engineering & Environmental Division, Highways Agency.

☐ THE answer given by Nigel Organ is indicative of the Highway Agency's casual attitude to road safety. By permitting vehicles to travel faster on rougher road surfaces, the more vulnerable road users, such as cyclists and pedestrians, are forced off the road and into using cars themselves. In countries which have a smoother road surface, traffic travels slower, road noise is reduced, and cyclists are encouraged to use the road both by the reduced vehicle speeds and the smoother riding surface, which incidentally is much kinder to a cyclist's skin if he/she falls off.
Tim Chamberlain, Bristol.

☐ THE real reason our roads are so bad is that they are laid with the cheaper wheel-suspended surface laying machines and not the tank-like track-laying machines that used to be used. The tracked machines perform a better averaging of the surface than the wheeled machines, leading to a much better macro surface.
A. A. Brodie, Finchley, London.

QUESTION: The trains from Paris to London will arrive at Waterloo Station. What would be a symmetrically tactless name for the station at which the London to Paris trains will arrive?

☐ GARE DE L'HASTINGS!
Alan Casey, Raunds, Northants.

☐ LA REINE THATCHER.
John Northeast, London NW1.

☐ How about the Gare Delors?
Andrew Smith, London.

☐ THERE is a problem with Alan Casey's suggestion: if the London to Paris train went to Hastings instead of the Gare du Nord, the train wouldn't cross the Channel.
Dan Wilson, Lewes, E. Sussex.

☐ THE station could also be named after Bouvines, a battle in which King John was hammered by Philippe Auguste (1214) of which very few English people have ever heard, but which led to Magna Carta the following year. Exactly 600 years later (1814), Bergen-op-Zoom was another humiliating defeat for the English. Three flags captured from British regiments may still be seen at Les Invalides in Paris. And at Fontenoy (1745) an Anglo-Dutch army commanded by the loathsome Duke of Cumberland was roundly defeated by the great Marshal Saxe.
Ralph Lloyd-Jones, East Dulwich, London SE22.

☐ I THINK 'Gare des Loos' would be appropriate.
C. A. Newton Appleton, Warrington.

☐ AIRLINE passengers disembarking at Charles de Gaulle will suspect that the French have already taken reciprocal action.
Alan Hooper, New Eltham, London SE9.

QUESTION: A friend carries an organ donor card to

**which he has added the words: 'My organs are not
to be used for a member of the Conservative Party.'
Would his wishes be respected? Would his estate have
any recourse if not?**

☐ EVEN though I agree entirely with the sentiment
expressed, we do not retrieve organs from anyone who
puts conditions on their use. Once removed, donor organs
are placed with recipients who have, in the opinion of
the transplant team, the best chance of success, both
short-term and long-term. This is regardless of race,
colour, religion or indeed political views. Your friend
should either tear up his donor card, or remove this
clause. The card has no legal status, and therefore no
recourse could be taken.
Deirdre M. Westwood, Transplant Coordinator, Nottingham.

☐ IF ANY one of my bits and pieces are ever transplanted
into a Conservative, it would reject them.
Allan Davies, Grimsby, S. Humberside.

☐ I WOULD hope that the carrier of this card (or his estate)
would have no legal recourse whatsoever for this ludicrous
action. Since the holder dislikes Conservatives so much he
is, presumably, a socialist. Is he therefore advocating a
medical system whereby patients are asked their political
affiliations before being treated? This is clearly some new
and exciting form of socialism I was not previously aware
of. I personally am proud that my regard for human life
extends beyond my party-political beliefs. Anyone (even
Tony Blur) is welcome to my organs after my death if it
will help to save a life.
Tim Walls, London SW7.

☐ LIKE Tim Walls, I would be happy to let a member of

the Conservative Party have any of my organs – at the
current market rate, of course.
Richard Towers, Lymm, Cheshire.

☐ MY LIVER is in an advanced state of cirrhosis, my
pancreas rotten with paracetamol and my kidneys pickled
in alcohol. My lungs are all glued together with the tar
from 30 years of 60 cigarettes a day; my stomach and
duodenum are riddled with ulcers; my eyes almost closed
with cataracts; and my optic nerves wasted with worry
about the rest. My heart only continues to beat with the
aid of a plastic contraption which holds the mitral valve
together. I absolutely insist that upon my demise every
one of my organs is transplanted in different members of
the Conservative Party, whether they like it or not. There
is no charge.
Gerard Mulholland, Chevilly-Larue, France.

**QUESTION: Can anyone tell me how to clean out the
inside of the yellow plastic ducks my children have
as bath toys? The kids have a habit of drinking out
of them.**

☐ ALTHOUGH it may take the fun out of bathtime, the
solution is to stop the ducks from getting soiled in the first
place. A warm soldering iron touched over the offending
holes should prevent the ducks from filling up and the
children from drinking the resulting grimy water. If, after
surgery, the ducks are *too* buoyant, may I suggest partially
filling the ducks with water before sealing them.
Dean Belfield, Warrington, Lancs.

☐ DEAN BELFIELD would reduce bathtime to a mere
ablution. The questioner should get some Chempro SPD
from a home-brewing shop. Mix a solution as directed

on the packet – about half a gallon should suffice – in a plastic bucket. Submerge the duck or ducks and fill them, as the children do for drinking and squirting. When full, leave submerged for 15 to 20 minutes. Drain and empty duck. Rinse inside and out with clean cold water. The duck will be both cleaned and sterilised and the process will not detract from the flavour of the bathwater. It has the added advantage of working equally well with plastic ducks of any other colour.
Alf Cornford, Sheffield.

□ IN THE short term the questioner should deny her children access to cups, mugs, glasses, beakers or bottles, and instead give them all their liquid requirements from plastic ducks. The long-term solution is to add at least six more children to her family in as short a time as possible. She will then find that their habit of drinking bathwater from plastic ducks, or indeed any other vessel, is the least of her worries.
Dorothy Harrison, Peverell, Plymouth.

□ APPLY a liberal amount of Stop'n'Grow anti-nail-biting polish around the holes. It tastes foul.
Jane Gallagher, Oxford.

QUESTION: Who founded the first merchant bank in London and when?

□ WHO *precisely* founded the first merchant bank is not known. But we do know that in 1157 the merchants of the Hanseatic League in London (resident at Dowgate on the north bank of the Thames between London Bridge and Cannon Street station in the so-called 'German House' or 'Steelyard') were licensed to lend money at interest to Henry II, one of the ablest of the English kings.

He needed cash 'to live of his own' and to finance his many wars at home and abroad (he also ruled about half of present-day France). These merchants, mostly from Cologne, were freed from all London tolls and customs and permitted to trade at fairs throughout England. The merchants of Lübeck and Hamburg, chartered in 1266 by Henry III, coalesced with the Cologne association in 1282 to become the most powerful Hanseatic colony in London, with houses at many other English ports.
Ray Boston, Cardiff.

☐ THE longest established of the existing London merchant banks is Barings plc. It was established on Christmas Day 1762 by two brothers as John and Francis Baring & Co.
Chris Moon, Chartered Institute of Bankers, London EC3.

QUESTION: I have seen the claim on fruit machines that they return a certain percentage of gamblers' stake money. Given the random chance element, how could a trading standards officer ever check such a claim?

☐ WHEN I was managing a club in Australia some years ago I conducted extensive research on some of the poker machines in use. These were of the mechanical 'one-armed bandit' type. Three drums each carried 16 cards, providing 4,096 combinations. By varying the number of aces, kings, etc., it was possible to increase or reduce the player's chances of winning – though it was more likely that small winnings would be re-inserted, while anyone winning the jackpot was more likely to stop playing. The results on 10,000 or more pulls were found to be almost exactly in accordance with the mathematical probability, though, as one might expect, the sequences were unpredictable. What was discovered was that too high a take discouraged players on a particular machine and reduced turnover. Too low a percentage was risky for the club and might fail to meet overheads (including the tax). Ten per cent of turnover was found to be the optimum gross profit margin. Most machines nowadays are electronically programmed and it is likely that their out-turn is even more predictable, though activities such as 'freezing' and 'nudging', which give the player the illusion of exercising skill, make the calculation more complex. Honouring promises of minimum return can easily be verified by comparing the meter showing the number of coins inserted with the residual cash over a period of time.

Malcolm McDougall, Hampton Wick, Kingston upon Thames, Surrey.

QUESTION: Can readers suggest any books likely to help a 45-year-old man who has spent 26 years in prison and who is now totally out of touch with modern life?

☐ PERHAPS it would be a good idea if he continued to be in touch with 1969, as by the time he has worked out what modern life is all about, it will have changed again. However, he could immerse himself in Richard Dawkins's *The Blind Watchmaker*, and have his eyes really opened to reality.

Len Clarke, Uxbridge, Middlx.

☐ THE best (and cheapest) thing for him to do is to strike up an acquaintance with a university student, and then join the student in long mornings (before the other students crowd the shared computers) surfing the Internet, paying particular attention to newsgroups like 'soc.culture.British'.

Larry Winger, Newcastle.

QUESTION: St Paul's Cathedral is said to have the second-largest unsupported dome in the world. What does this mean, and is it true?

☐ AN UNSUPPORTED dome on a building is one which has no additional supports, such as central pillars or columns, and is held up purely by the fabric of the dome itself. That on St Paul's Cathedral is 112 feet in diameter, but is smaller than the dome of the British Museum's reading room, which has a diameter of 140 feet and a capacity of 1.25 million cubic feet. The dome is held up by cast-iron ribs within its structure.
Ian Lawther, Faversham, Kent.

☐ ST PAUL'S is not a 'true' dome, but rather a copper-clad roof supported on a conically shaped truss work of timbers. In turn, this sits upon a stone 'drum'. Sir Christopher Wren was aware that this set-up would collapse under its own weight and therefore tied it together by setting a chain around the drum – bracelet-like. The inner 'dome' (more correctly a ceiling) is suspended from above.
Munroe Hall, Bury.

☐ MUNROE HALL may well be correct in saying that the apparent 'dome' of St Paul's is not a true dome, in the narrow structural sense, but in doing so he has raised a few red herrings. The outer covering is lead, not copper. The cone, which is the primary structure, is brick, not timber – what appear to be timber trusses are merely struts forming the external shape of the 'dome' (which is purely cosmetic) bracketed off the cone. The inner dome, which is also largely cosmetic, is not suspended but is self-supporting, and is therefore a true dome. The primary purpose of the brick cone is to support the heavy

lantern at the top of the 'dome'. The chain is at the base of the cone, which coincides with the springing of the inner dome and the top of the drum; there it resists the tendency of both cone and dome to spread laterally. The inner part of the drum is also slightly conical, above the Whispering Gallery, in order to create an effect of greater height by false perspective. I believe that Christopher Wren thought that the structure would be stable without the chain, but put one in nevertheless. Between the two world wars, it was found necessary to insert further chains. The structure of the dome is illustrated in Bannister Fletcher's *History of Architecture*.
John Roberts, Llandysul, Dyfed.

☐ THE figures given of 112 feet in diameter for St Paul's and 140 feet for the British Museum reading room, are both outdone by the unsupported dome of Rome's Pantheon. Still in perfect condition, of un-reinforced lime concrete and erected nearly 1,900 years ago, its diameter is 142½ feet.
Len Clarke, Denham, Uxbridge, Middlx.

☐ THE Devonshire Royal Hospital was originally built in 1790 by the Duke of Devonshire as stabling for horses. In 1857 a portion of the stabling block and surrounding land was given over as a hospital. The magnificent slate dome was added in 1880 and at that time was the largest unsupported dome in the world with a span of 154 feet.
J. Tatum, Buxton, Derby.

QUESTION: Descartes said that the only thing that is certain is the existence of doubt. How could he be so sure?

☐ HE WASN'T. That's why he was.
David Boland, Wanstead, London E11.

☐ DESCARTES didn't say this. At an early stage of his antisceptical project, after subjecting all his beliefs to an artificial and exaggerated doubt, he realised that he could at least be certain of his own existence. One reason for this was that if he doubted that he existed, then he must exist in order to do the doubting. He went on to try to re-establish all of his former beliefs as certain – in which he thought he'd succeeded. Descartes thus believed that a vast number of beliefs are certain. The question as asked seems to assume that there is a contradiction involved in doubting everything except doubt itself. Does the questioner think that doubtful doubt is the same as certainty?
Peter J. King, St Hilda's College, Oxford.

☐ DESCARTES'S residual certainty was 'thinking': '*Cogito, ergo sum*'. The fallacy was that Descartes thought he had reduced his sceptical investigation to one element only, and he overlooked his assumption that there was a second: the 'I' in 'I think, therefore I am'. He fails to subject 'I' to his own sceptical process. This 'I' led to dualist philosophy and the soul in the pineal gland, but he never proves that 'I' is an entity rather than a generalised term for consciousness.
Karl Heath, Coventry.

☐ 'I AM confused, therefore I am' might be a more relevant argument for Karl Heath. He suggests that for Descartes the soul is in the pineal gland, whereas Descartes concludes that the soul has no spatial location, being neither in nor outside nor above nor below the pineal gland. Descartes usually is uncertain about those beliefs which he could conceivably doubt or over which he could make a mistake.

So, when Peter King tells us that Descartes realised that he could be certain of his existence because, in doubting, he must exist in order to do the doubting, there is some confusion. It is impossible both for Descartes to believe he thinks or exists and be mistaken in his belief; but it looks as if this is being confused with the mistaken claim that it is impossible for Descartes to doubt or make a mistake about these matters. His reflections on the possibility of an evil genius, for example, could lead him into mistakenly thinking that he does not exist or is not thinking. Heavy alcoholic consumption could have the same outcome. As it is, it seems as if he thinks he cannot make a mistake about his existence, thus making a mistake.
Peter Cave, Hampstead, London NW3.

QUESTION: Why was Army punishment known as jankers?

□ ERIC PARTRIDGE'S *Dictionary of Slang* places the first appearance of this term just before world war one and links it to an obsolete form of 'jangle', meaning to complain. Hence, a 'jankers man' is a defaulter and a 'jankers king' a provost sergeant.
Peter Barnes, Simpson, Bucks.

QUESTION: Where is the remotest place in mainland Britain and what is the best criterion for making a decision?

□ POSSIBLY the remotest habitation is Scorraig, on the south side of Loch Broom neighbouring Ullapool. Scorraig can be reached on foot only via a difficult path which edges around the hillside on the south side of the peninsula. Most of the locals and visitors would rather cross by boat: there is

limited public access by the 'ferry service' so if you need to go there it's best to make alternative arrangements. For the test of 'remoteness', ask a parcel courier who guarantees overnight mainland delivery by 9 a.m. to include Scorraig and then rank the resulting excuses.
Kim Birkhead, Wrexham, Clwyd.

☐ IT MUST be 10 Downing Street – it's certainly the furthest from reality!
David J. Gadd, Pagham, W. Sussex.

QUESTION: Why does a pepper pot have about five holes and a salt pot only one?

☐ ACCORDING to old-fashioned etiquette books, pepper is sprinkled over the food, but salt is put in a small heap at one side of the plate and each forkful dipped in it. Hence the now old-fashioned salt-cellar, a small dish full of salt with a small salt spoon. Only in relatively recent times has salt become free-flowing (by the use of appropriate additives) and so usable in a pot rather than a cellar.
D. Broadbent, Manchester.

☐ AT A lunch I had in Brussels last year, six European nationals were around the table; three of them expected salt to emerge from a pot with a single hole and three expected pepper to emerge. In view of the damage that this may make (every day) to food, shouldn't the European Commission insist on them all being standardised?
David Flanders, Chorley, Lancs.

☐ A PEPPER pot should have *exactly* five holes. Anything else is a calculated insult to Sir Thomas Browne on the perfection of the quincunx (one dot at each corner and one in the centre), who designed the first pepper pot

accordingly. He was not a user of salt and left the design of the first salt pot to his assistant, the laziest scoundrel ever, who from sheer idleness made one hole and left it at that.
Brian Birch, Cottingham, N. Humberside.

QUESTION: Is there an opposite to paranoia, i.e. being under the mistaken belief that everyone is out to help you?

☐ YES; Annekariceonoia.
Susan Peak, Ashton-under-Lyne, Lancs.

☐ IT'S called 'canvassing'.
Liz Cullen, Malmesbury, Wilts.

☐ THE most obvious opposite of paranoia is pronoia, or the delusion that everyone loves you. Most agree this affliction is common among performance artists, politicians, social workers and teachers, but I gather that this condition is rarely treatable as the sufferers rarely believe that they have a problem. On the other hand, the mistaken belief that everyone wants to help you is best described as parasitism.
Kaktus Leach, Sheffield.

QUESTION: Is it morally right for a lawyer to defend a client despite knowing that the client is guilty?

☐ YES – although the nature of the defence must be clarified. If the client tells us that he/she is guilty, there are two ways of 'defending' the case. The first is upon a guilty plea, defending a client's interests by way of mitigation. Secondly, a client may be defended by getting the prosecution to prove its allegation. It is morally right that the state should be required to prove its case against those whom it seeks to prosecute. To allow anything less than proof would be wholly unacceptable. This process of 'putting to proof' is closely connected to the issue of the right to silence. Any legal right or freedom is a building block in the overall morality of a society, even when such a right or freedom may enable the individual to act with something short of full personal morality.

Tim Rose (defence solicitor), Douglas & Partners, Bristol.

□ No. THE principles under which I have operated as a criminal defence lawyer for the last 24 years have been as follows: If the client says that he is not guilty, then I accept at face value his instructions, and I will 'defend' him to the best of my ability. If the evidence against him is so overwhelming that he will be convicted in any event, I will always point out clearly the risks that he faces, but the decision must always be that of the client. If he persists in his denial, then I will continue to defend him. If a client tells me that he is guilty, but he is going to put forward a defence, I will show him the door forthwith. If a client admits to me his guilt and subsequently admits it to the court, I have no moral qualm at all about representing him (not 'defending him'), so that all that is good about him (if anything) can be said to the court.

Roger Corbett, Russell Jones & Walker, Birmingham.

QUESTION: Is Buckfastleigh the longest place name with no repeated letters?

□ BUSLINGTHORPE, a hamlet in north Lincolnshire, equals Buckfastleigh.

Rosalind Boyce, Market Rasen, Lincs.

☐ I HAVE always believed that the longest is the village of Bricklehampton in Worcestershire.
Moira Thelwell, Bolsterstone, Sheffield.

☐ SOUTH FAMBRIDGE, Essex.
J. C. Hall, Southport, Merseyside.

QUESTION: Which is the safest method of transport (i.e. ship, bus, train, car)?

☐ THE Department of Transport's annual publication *Transport Statistics Great Britain* gives this information. Different modes of transport are used for different purposes, but the overall averages show that air has the lowest fatality rate at 0.3 per billion kilometres travelled. This is followed by bus and coach at 0.4, rail 1, car 4, ship 6 and motorbike 100. Figures are for travel in Britain, except for air and water which are for travel in UK-registered aircraft or vessels. If account is taken of serious injuries also, rail is safer than bus or coach.
D. W. Flaxen, DoT, London SW1.

☐ THE figures given, based on a common mileage, indicate that air travel is the safest mode of transport. However, if the calculation were based upon a common *time* (e.g. an hour in a plane, an hour in a car, etc.) the same figures would yield a rather different order of safety: Bus/coach 0.25 units; rail 1; air 2.25; ship 2.25; car 3; motorbike 75. On this basis a day's flight is nine times more likely to prove fatal than a day's coach journey. Who is to say which criterion is the more valid?
P. W. French, Farnham, Surrey.

☐ WALKING. Last year pedestrians killed no one in a bus or a lorry. But buses and lorries, the most dangerous form of road transport, killed 195 pedestrians; cars and vans killed another 1,016. D. W. Flaxen of the Department of Transport answers from the perspective of the motorist – demonstrating, despite some recent green rhetoric, where the Department's heart is still to be found. But statistics can tell only part of the story. There were fewer than half as many children killed in road accidents last year than in the early 1920s. This does not prove that it has become twice as safe for children to play in the street; it suggests that parental appreciation of the threat of traffic is now so great that they don't allow their children out any more.

John Adams, Geography Department, University College London.

QUESTION: UK bank notes are merely IOUs, since they carry the words: 'I promise to pay the bearer on demand the sum of . . .' signed by the Governor of the Bank of England. How can I cash this IOU, and in what form would it be paid?

☐ THIS wording is simply a relic of the days when the country was still using the gold standard. The pound note was supposed to represent a pound's-worth of gold deposited in the vaults of the Bank of England for which, in theory at least, it could at any time be exchanged. But nowadays, if money no longer represents an entitlement to a given quantity of gold, then precisely what is it? Conventional economists say that money cannot be accurately defined, which is distinctly odd since money is an artefact, entirely a creation of man. Bankers on the other hand seem to take a different view. In his book *Money in Britain*, R. S. Sayer tells us that money has no intrinsic value and that we now have a commodity-based currency instead of one based on gold. That is, the value of money lies in that it can be exchanged for the commodities and

services which the real economy produces. But if the value of money is dependent upon the productive capacity of the real economy, then financial or fiscal measures designed to impair the productive capacity of the real economy to preserve the value of the currency must, in reality, be self-defeating.
T. W. Parsons, Twickenham, Middlx.

□ T. W. PARSON'S reply omitted two points.
1. Bank notes are not IOUs, which are merely records of debts, but are promissory notes, promising specific repayment as stated.
2. The Catch 22 is that you could sue the Governor for the amount on your bank note, and win. But he will legally redeem his promise with another bank note for the same amount.
W. W. Bloomfield, Camberley, Surrey.

□ THE IOU on the currency notes can be redeemed in whatever form you wish. If you want it in gold then the man at Threadneedle Street could direct you to a jeweller or bullion dealer who would be only too happy to complete the transaction. Alternatively, you can convert it into company shares, Big Macs or whatever takes your fancy. You can even cut out the middleman and go directly to the traders without bothering the Bank of England at all. The promise on the note should mean that the Bank will maintain the value of the currency. Whether or not it does that is another matter entirely.
Derek Middleton, Swinton, S. Yorks.

QUESTION: What is the origin of the term 'dumb-bells'?

□ THE term was originally used for an apparatus like that

for ringing a church bell (but without the bell itself – hence 'dumb'), employed in body exercises. In the *Spectator* (1711), Addison describes how he took exercise every morning upon such an instrument, and said that his landlady and her daughters did not dare to disturb him while he was 'ringing'. John Wesley in 1784 suggested similar exercise 'if you cannot ride or walk abroad'. It gradually came to be used in our sense of an exercising weight consisting of a single bar weighted with a heavy ball or disc at either end, used in pairs, grasped with the hands and swung for exercise. Other meanings include a similar-shaped microscopic crystal found in the urine, a nebula in the constellation Vulpecula, a wooden object used for a dog to return, and (in American and Canadian slang) a fool.

B. C. Morgan, Uppingham, Rutland.

QUESTION: I once read that the Americans had intercepted several radio transmissions made by dying Russian cosmonauts before Gagarin's successful spaceflight. Any confirmation?

☐ Copies of *The Guinness Book of Records* printed in the early 1960s contained a list of 'Soviet space fatalities' from *c.*1957 to 1960. On various dates, named cosmonauts were alleged to have asphyxiated, gone mad in orbit, burned up on re-entry, survived but been consigned to mental institutions etc. I have never seen mention of this list or these 'facts' anywhere else. *Glasnost* within the Soviet space programme and eager digging by Western journalists should have revealed a pattern of disaster by now if any existed. I assume the editors of the *Book of Records* were fed a straight piece of anti-Soviet propaganda and fell for it.

J. T. Brooks, Rogerstone, Gwent.

□ *THE GUINNESS BOOK OF RECORDS*, 1965, lists at least nine cosmonauts who preceded Gagarin. It states: 'Persistent reports, even from Communist sources, before and after Gagarin's feat, allege that Lt Col. Vladimir Illyushin had made one voluntary and two further involuntary orbits of the Earth during 9 April 1961, and had become mentally deranged. These reports were officially but not conclusively refuted on 1 May 1961. Italian agency reports and others maintain that at least nine men from the USSR preceded Gagarin in manned rocket launches, but with fatal results.'
Paul E. Murphy, Rathgar, Dublin.

QUESTION: 'As happy as Larry'. Why Larry?

□ THE term is probably derived from 'As Happy as a Lark' where lark is a recent adaptation of the dialect *lake* meaning sport and Old English *lac* meaning contest. According to *Brewer's Dictionary*, Larry comes from the Australian word Larrikin meaning a street rowdy which in turn derives from the Irish pronunciation of 'larking'. Brewer also suggests that the original Larry may have been Larry Foley (1847–1917) a noted Australian boxer.
Brian Palmer, Noke Side, St Albans, Herts.

QUESTION: What area of land given over to wind farming would produce the power-generating capacity of each of the four main fuels: coal, gas, oil and nuclear?

□ WIND farms in the UK are typically based on separation distances of between five and 10 times the diameter of the turbine rotor. A wind farm of 10 turbines with typical rotor diameters could extend over about 50 hectares (e.g.

a rectangle of 100 metres by 500 metres). The precise spacing depends on the wind regime over the site. But this represents purely the external boundaries of the wind farm. The actual land 'given over' to the turbines (and the accompanying access roads) is much less than this – typically only 1 or 2 per cent of the area of the wind farm – because normal agricultural activities can continue right up to the base of the turbines. A crude assessment, looking at just the amount of land required by wind farms to match the output of other power stations, would yield the following: The average rated capacity of coal-fired plants in England and Wales is 1,164 MW (which would supply about 4 per cent of the UK's electricity demand). This could be matched by about 180 wind farms occupying about 270 hectares but extending over some 27,000 hectares. To put this into context, there are some 18,500,000 million hectares used for agriculture and the Government estimates that it is reasonable for the UK to get some 10 per cent of its electricity from the wind by the early part of next century.

Michael Harper, Director, British Wind Energy Association, London WC2.

□ WHY use land? With the construction technology used to build oil rigs in the sea, we could site all the windmills we need in mid-Atlantic, where there's plenty of wind and no one to complain about the noise or view.

Rachel Johnston, Keighley, W. Yorks.

□ IF THERE were a day with little or no wind, the entire area of the British Isles and associated territorial waters would have to be given over to wind generators to produce nothing. Hence wind power is prohibitively expensive, except as a minor adjunct to an already complete and self-contained electrical system. Power stations must be ready to supply electrical energy when required irrespective of whether the wind be blowing or not, and so any number of wind generators can never be used as a replacement for even a single power station. The only savings that can be made are on the power station fuel costs, but these are significantly less than the total electricity costs, typically 2–3p per unit (kWh), which should be compared with the 11p per unit given to the wind generators; quite a subsidy.

W. M. Nelis (C. Eng., MIEE), Porthmadog, Gwynedd.

□ MICHAEL HARPER'S answer contains dubious figures. The wind farms in Cornwall have shown that each 400kW turbine (a typical size) produces about one million units per year. The total UK electrical power consumption was 280 TWh (280,000 million units) in 1992. Therefore to produce just 4 per cent of this (i.e. 11,200 million units) will require 11,200 wind generators, and at the rate of 50 hectares per 10 generators will extend over an area of 56,000 hectares (i.e. 216 square miles). The 'reasonable estimate' of 10 per cent from the wind by the early part of the next century will require 28,000 turbines covering an area of 540 square miles – a mile-wide swathe of wind generators stretching 500 miles from Cornwall to Cumbria!

E. W. Luscombe (C. Eng., MIEE), Stoke, Devon.

QUESTION: What does Acas do between strikes?

□ ACAS works very hard to prevent strikes! The aim of the service is to conciliate between parties in dispute before any industrial action occurs, on the basis that prevention is better than cure. Acas is proud of its record – in over 90 per cent of completed conciliation cases all forms of industrial action have been avoided. In recent years the number of industrial stoppages has fallen dramatically but the demand for Acas conciliation has remained fairly constant. In 1993 Acas received just over 1,200 requests for conciliation. Another major element of Acas's work is to try to resolve individual employment rights complaints before they go to an industrial tribunal hearing. A record 75,000 of these individual conciliation cases were dealt with in 1993, with only one-third having to be heard by a tribunal; almost one million of these cases have been handled by Acas since its inception in 1974. Acas also provides a nationwide telephone enquiry service supplying information on employment-related matters. Almost half a million people used it last year.

John Hougham, Chairman, Acas, London SW1.

QUESTION: When did the western world start using 'Anno Domini' to show which year it was; what form of registering years was in common use before then?

☐ THE way of registering years in most places was to count from the accession of the king or, in a republic, to give the names of annual officials (archons in Athens, consuls in Rome). Civilisations covering large areas for long periods also adopted eras, counting from some mythical or historical event: the four-year cycle of Olympic Games from 776 BC; the foundation of Rome in 753 BC; the establishment of the Seleucid dynasty in 312 BC. The early Christians adopted the Roman system, using years of Emperors, Olympiads and the foundation of Rome, and also the 15-year cycle of tax indictions established in the Roman Empire in AD 297 (still used in the Church). They also added years of Bishops and in some places adopted the era of Martyrs from AD 284. But as Christianity lasted and expanded, several scholars tried to compile universal chronologies, dating from the Creation of the World (between 6000 and 4000 BC) or the calling of Abraham (about 2000 BC). In the early 6th century, the Roman scholar Dionysius Exiguus suggested counting years from the Incarnation of Jesus, fixing the Conception on 25 March and the Nativity on 25 December AD 1 (four years after the death of Herod and five years before the Census in Judea). This system slowly spread through western Europe, taken on by Bede in the early 8th century and officially adopted by the Emperor Charlemagne in the 9th century. It then spread throughout the world, becoming the Common Era with years counted as CE or BCE. The Jewish era counts from the Creation in 3761 BC, and the Muslim era from the Hijra in AD 622. The Renaissance scholar Scalliger collated all chronologies in a Julian era from 4713 BC (used by astronomers and historians), and the French Revolutionaries tried to establish a Republican era from 1792.

Nicolas Walter, Islington, London N1.

QUESTION: Are humans the only animal to overeat and become fat?

☐ No, ALTHOUGH in many animals food intake is closely matched to energy expenditure. Goldfish, for example will reduce the amount they eat if the water temperature is reduced, causing a reduction in their overall metabolic rate. A study in which laboratory rats were given an assortment of palatable supermarket foods ('cafeteria feeding') led to overeating and obesity in about 40 per cent of the animals. Exercise reduced the amount of weight gain in males but, curiously, had no effect on the weight gain in female rats in the same study. Spontaneous obesity has been observed in some primates and it can certainly be induced in captive monkeys if they are given a diet high in fat and sucrose. It is important to remember that overeating (hyperphagia) is not the only

factor involved. Obesity may go along with normal food intake, for example where there is reduced bodily activity or where a genetic predisposition to overweight exists as it does in at least some pigs.
Michael Hutton, Camberwell, London SE5.

☐ CATS, dogs, hamsters, gerbils, rats, rabbits, cows, pigs, chickens, sheep, gorillas, goldfish, bats, chinchillas and tapeworms can all overeat. Humans may be the only animals to diet, however.
Daniel Norcross, London SW17.

QUESTION: What are the origins of the well-known scout campfire song 'Ging gang gooly gooly gooly gooly wacha gin gan goo . . . ?' What do the words mean?

☐ IT IS possibly a translation of the chorus of this Spanish song (the tune is the same): *Ing gan gollo gollo gollo gollo . . . Ing gan go . . .* One of its verses translates as:

> When a Chinese girl gets married in Japan,
> The next day they paint her with coal,
> The next day someone dances with her.
> It's a very refined dance that will result.

Geo Jenner and Sonia Falces, Luxembourg.

☐ WHEN I was a scout, I was told the 'ging-gang' song had been created at the first Jamboree of scouts by combining words from the languages of every country represented.
Alan Paterson, London N16.

QUESTION: By what right can the British State require me to observe its laws and accept its institutions, given

that I have never been asked to signify my assent to arrangements which include ones negotiated in previous generations by tiny elites?

☐ IF YOU have ever made use of the provisions of British law yourself, it could be argued that you have implicitly consented to comply with the entire body of it. But it is easier to argue that you imply consent when you participate in the democratic process by voting. This may also be the principle that leads opposition parties to withdraw from elections when they think they will be rigged; by not putting up candidates, and by asking their supporters to abstain, they presumably hope to invalidate the government's claims on them for compliance, freeing them and their supporters to oppose the Government both within and outside the law. But even this latter argument for compliance seems rather stretched; many people comply but don't vote; and many people who vote are none the less outraged at some of the legislation they are asked to comply with. Rights are things you get when they are granted to you. You have no rights (in law) other than those granted to you, and conversely the State's rights over you can only be the rights you have granted to it. *John Cleaver, London.*

☐ JOHN CLEAVER'S answer is not entirely satisfactory. If the State has no rights over an individual without their consent, then it can have no right to control the actions of most people under the age of 18, since it does not allow such people to vote, nor does it ensure that they have the opportunity to consent in any other way. This would imply, for instance, that the only reasonable way to remove a 12-year-old playing on a railway line would be through impact with a train. Any answer to the question should take into account that a state is not only an abstract entity: it also implicates huge numbers of individuals, in part through the existence of consensus. For example, when police officers restrict an individual's liberty by preventing him or her from driving the wrong way up a motorway, their action frequently draws the approbation of a majority of onlookers. These onlookers wish this aspect of State activity to continue. There does not seem to be any reason why their wishes should not be accorded at least as much respect as the wishes of dissidents who would prefer to be free to drive on the right if they want to, like other Europeans. Readers might conclude that while the majority is perhaps not always right, doing what it wants – obeying the state, for example – does violate the wishes of fewer people.

Hudson Pace, Teddington, Middlx.

☐ TOM PAINE, in his *Rights of Man*, 1791, supplied an answer to this question. 'There never did, there never will, and there never can exist a parliament, or any description of men, or any generation of men, in any country, possessed of the right or the power of binding and controlling postcrity to the "end of time", or of commanding for ever how the world shall be governed, or who shall govern it; and therefore, all such clauses, acts or declarations, by which the makers of them attempt to do what they have neither the right nor the power to do, nor the power to execute, are in themselves null and void. Every age and generation must be as free to act for itself, in all cases, as the ages and generations which preceded it. The vanity and presumption of governing beyond the grave, is the most ridiculous and insolent of all tyrannies. Man has no property in man; neither has any generation a property in the generations which are to follow.'

John Davies, History Department, Liverpool Institute of Higher Education.

☐ QUESTIONS on the nature of the individual, their moral

fibre and their rights were argued about at length during the 18th and 19th centuries. John Stuart Mill argued for utilitarianism, of which the founding principle was that 'society' was more important than any one person or group of individuals. So individuals had the right to do as they pleased, provided they did not impinge upon the rights of others. There was also a theory that just and otherwise law-abiding people, of suitable moral rectitude, were within their rights to disregard laws they considered inherently unjust. This presupposes that 'good' citizens do not need laws to keep them in check. Thus, individuals are not going to object to a directive or law which prohibits something which they would never dream of doing anyway. All the theories on law and moral development were developed when the law was so draconian that society was effectively lawless – if you are going to hang, you may as well commit a big crime. Today we may consider that some laws which exist from those times are petty, but they rarely result in conviction. And we may think that some sentences passed by judges are ridiculous, or that their comments show a lack of understanding, but this does not necessarily undermine the authority of the law or our obligation to obey it.

Graham R. Jones, Withington, Manchester.

☐ MANY are the political philosophers who have tried to turn the fact that humans are social animals into some ethical or pseudo-scientific basis for the injunction to observe laws. But as any good anarchist knows, by the right of might is the true answer to this question. The fact that it is sensible or desirable to have some rules and to obey them, such as traffic rules, does not give generalised grounds for observing all laws. Each of us has the right, even the duty, to question the laws imposed on us. In some forms of direct democracy, individuals have the chance to acquiesce deliberately in the rules that are

generated to govern the society to which they belong, and to argue for changes or new ones. In the so-called representative so-called democracies, we are powerless and allow institutions to frighten us into obedience. Their 'right' is our 'duty'. While the sanction of punishment for breaking laws is undoubtedly one reason why many people are law-abiding, the really clever bit is the fear that is conditioned into us – a fear that makes us delegate our power as individuals to the State, and lets us duck the moral responsibility for our actions.
Maurice Herson, Oxford.

QUESTION: When the sun or moon is setting, its reflection in the sea appears as a narrow band reaching to the horizon. Is there a name for this effect – and a simple explanation?

☐ THE surface of the ocean is always dimpled into myriads of dome-shaped 'wavelets'. At sunset, the sunbeams skim over the sea horizontally and are reflected off every wavelet that is high enough to 'see' the setting sun. Sunbeams can reach our eyes by glancing off the crests of all those wavelets that lie between us and the horizon, immediately below the disc of the sun. The top of each wavelet acts as a small horizontal convex mirror, which glints in the sunlight as it deflects the sunbeam very slightly upwards to our eyes. The required vertical deflection is so small, even for close wavelets, that the ray of light is still travelling almost horizontally until it reaches us, on the shore. The situation is different for a sunbeam reflected from a wavelet that is not exactly between us and the sun. If, for example, the wavelet is one degree out of line, the sunlight travels horizontally until it reaches the off-axis wavelet. There, it must be reflected towards our eyes through one degree. However, this reflection must take place in an almost horizontal plane for the sunbeam to stand any chance of reaching our eyes, which are nearly at sea-level. When a sunbeam hits a wavelet it suffers a vertical deflection and passes high over our heads, so we don't see the setting sun glinting on the waves, except immediately below the sun's disc. When the sun is high in the sky, the wavelets are able to reflect the sunbeams back to our eyes through much larger angles, so a wide expanse of ocean can sparkle in the midday sunshine.

Roger W. Kersey, consultant physicist, Nutley, E. Sussex.

QUESTION: Is there an expert on photogravure and collegravure left in Britain? Can anyone help to identify, authenticate and advise on books about its early techniques?

□ BY FAR the best book on photogravure is *Photogravure* by H. Mills Cartwright (American Photographic Publishing Co., 1939). With regard to collegravure, I presume this is an obscure name for collotype, and the best book on this process is *The Practice of Collotype* (American Photographic Publishing Co., 1935). A book which covers both processes in very broad terms is *The Keepers of Light* by William Crawford (Morgan and Morgan, Dobbs Ferry, New York). This book is out of print at the moment, but it can be ordered from a local library. The last company I know of who were printing by the photogravure process were Vandyck Printers, Park Row, Bristol.

Keith Dugdale, Penzance, Cornwall.

□ COLLOGRAVURE, normally known as collography, is the collotype process adapted from flat glass plate to a film base wrapped around a cylinder. Collotype is to collography as photogravure is to rotogravure, and hand photogravure was also known as heliogravure. Because of confusion with

the mechanical process, the term rotogravure was used for press cylinder work and, like collotype and collography, to separate the flat-bed manual process from the rotary machine web-fed process. Neither is regarded as work of original graphic art because they both require preliminary photography. Both use collodion: photogravure (1869) is an intaglio process while collotype (1855) is relief or surface. Collotype is very expensive, with prints, often reproducing lithography, more valuable than the originals – and highly collected. It is not used for books. In collotype the trichromatic principle is not applicable, with five to eight or more workings needed for the full-colour effects for reproducing paintings. It depends entirely on the skill of the craftsperson. The weight and quality of paper is also significant in gravure processes. Photogravure began as a closely guarded secret known only to a few firms. Elaborate and intricate, it is capable of high-volume runs of fine quality and thus ideal for art books and glossy periodicals. Collography was rarely used for high-quantity production, but it is a rotary process, for which there were commercial applications. Both were largely superseded by photolithography – even by those retaining 'gravure' in their trading names – and in turn by digital techniques. Suggested books: Felix Brunner, *Handbook of Graphic Reproduction Processes* (Tirani, 1964); Harold Curwen, *Processes of Graphic Reproduction in Printing* (Faber, 1947); Thomas Griffiths, *Technique of Colour Printing by Lithography* (Faber, 1940); Sean Jennet, *The Making of Books* (Faber & Faber, 1951); J. C. Tarr, *Printing Today* (OUP, 1945). Libraries: London School of Printing; St Brides Institute of Printing; Watford College of Technology.
Ralph Gee, Nottingham.

☐ BAMBER GASCOIGNE wrote an excellent book on the subject, which is still in print. The Hunterian Art Gallery at the University of Glasgow also has a publication, and

has revolving exhibitions of its huge print collection with explanatory notes.
Martin Watt, Aberdeen.

QUESTION: What are the Seven Pillars of Wisdom? Proverbs 9 (from which T. E. Lawrence took his book title) gives only the first (the fear of God).

☐ THIS is another name for the Seven Gifts of the Spirit, or Holy Ghost. They are: Wisdom, Understanding, Counsel, Fortitude, Knowledge, Righteousness, Fear of the Lord. See *Brewer's Dictionary of Phrase and Fable.*
Frank Pashley, Chelmsford, Essex.

☐ THE Seven Pillars of Wisdom is a sandstone block at the entrance to Wadi Rum in southern Jordan. Thrust vertically nearly 1,000 feet by volcanic intrusion, erosion and faulting has produced seven apparent pillars. Wadi Rum became a favourite retreat for Lawrence and the Howeitat after attacks on the Damascus–Medina railway. Further into the wadi, there is a spring still known locally as Lawrence's Spring. In *Revolt in the Desert*, Lawrence describes his first sight of the Seven Pillars: 'We looked up on the left to a long wall of rock, sheering in like a thousand-foot wave towards the middle of the valley; whose other arc, to the right, was an opposing line of steep, red, broken hills . . . Our little caravan grew self-conscious, and fell dead quiet, afraid and ashamed to flaunt its smallness in the presence of the stupendous hills.' Camera teams were helicoptered to the tops of the cliffs, including the Seven Pillars, to film *Lawrence of Arabia*. Nowadays, tourists are driven at breakneck speed along the floor of the valley to see beautiful rock formations, sweeps of sand in subtle colours and Nabataean and pre-Nabataean rock carvings.
David Spilsbury, Cannon Hill, Birmingham.

☐ I WAS surprised by the explanations given. I had always thought that T. E. Lawrence had himself explained its origin. Shortly before the first world war he undertook a lengthy journey through the Middle East, visiting Classical and historical sites to write a book about the principal ancient cities of the region. He selected seven cities and chose the title 'Seven Pillars of Wisdom' to reflect their eminence in culture and learning. The book was never written because of the outbreak of the war in 1914. When he came to write his later work he simply used the title he had intended for the earlier unwritten book. He may of course have taken the phrase consciously or unconsciously from the Book of Proverbs.
R. Bartlett, London SW4.

QUESTION: Is it true that Queen's 'Bohemian Rhapsody' was a tribute to the 17-year-old Jewish homosexual Herschel Grynszpan, who assassinated a diplomat at Germany's Paris embassy – which caused the events of Kristallnacht? And whatever happened to Grynszpan?

☐ OF COURSE! That's what 'Scaramouche! Scaramouche! Will you do the fandango?' means. It all makes sense now. Any takers on 'Bismillah'?
Tim Footman, London SW4.

☐ I DON'T know about 'Bohemian Rhapsody', but Grynszpan's action moved the English composer Sir Michael Tippett to write an arrangement entitled *A Child of our Time*, portraying the suffering of the young Jew. However, after Grynszpan assassinated Ernst Vom Rath, the third secretary at Germany's Paris embassy, on 7 November 1938, his plight is a mystery. Grynszpan, a

Polish Jew living in Paris, made no attempt to escape and was immediately arrested. Vom Rath died from two gunshot wounds two days later, and Grynszpan was then charged with his murder. He was held in the Sachsenhausen concentration camp, where he was well treated, while Goebbels prepared a massive show trial. But when Grynszpan declared that he would use the trial to reveal his homosexual relationship with Vom Rath, the plan was abandoned. He somehow escaped immediate execution and survived Nazi custody until 30 January 1945 when, as prisoner 352044, he was liberated from the Magdeburg concentration camp by Allied troops. It is reported that Grynszpan then disappeared into France and was never heard of again. On 1 June 1960 his father obtained a declaration from the Hanover County Court that Herschel was officially dead, although the court had declined to make such a declaration on previous occasions due to lack of evidence. Two years later his elderly father was taken from his Israeli kibbutz to a concert hall in Haifa to hear a performance of Sir Michael Tippett's tribute. He died two weeks later.

David Northmore, Muswell Hill, London N10.

☐ GOEBBELS'S *Diaries* (edited Lochner, 1948) indicate that Goebbels was *not* in charge of Grynszpan's proposed German trial but was trying to hone in on the German Ministry of Justice's handling of it. According to Lochner, the alleged homosexuality of Grynszpan was Nazi-inspired propaganda. On 5 April 1942 Goebbels wrote: 'Grynszpan until now had always claimed, and rightly so, that he did not even know the [man] he shot. Now there is in existence some sort of anonymous letter by a Jewish refugee, which hints at the likelihood of homosexual intercourse between Grynszpan and Vom Rath. It is an absurd, typically Jewish, claim. The Ministry of Justice, however, did not hesitate to incorporate it in the indictment which was sent to the defendant.' It would seem Vom Rath was under *German* surveillance at the time, as a suspect anti-Nazi. Evidence of any homosexual liaison would certainly have been available to the Ministry of Justice in 1942. There seems never to have been any. Grynszpan's real motives were well known. His parents had been deported, with 17,000 other Jews, to Poland in October 1938. Poland had refused to let them in. They were stranded, in appalling conditions, in no man's land. Finally, Gerald Reitlinger in *Final Solution* (1971), quoting a New York German publication, *Aufban*, says Grynszpan was still alive in 1957, in Paris.

J. S. Brennan, Inverness.

QUESTION: If a king of England were to die leaving a pregnant wife and a surviving daughter, would the daughter inherit the throne or would we have to wait for the birth of a possible male heir?

☐ I HAVE read that, on the death of George VI, it was necessary to establish that Queen Elizabeth (now the Queen Mother) was not pregnant before proclaiming Princess Elizabeth queen, as a yet unborn child, if male, would have taken precedence at birth over the Heiress Presumptive.

A. H. Stafford, Marlow, Bucks.

QUESTION: The term 'Jim Crow' refers to the social, political and educational segregation of the races in 19th- and early 20th-century America, particularly in the southern states. Can anyone tell me who Jim Crow was?

☐ THOMAS DARTMOUTH 'DADDY' RICE (1808–1860) is

given credit, if such it is, for establishing the black-face characterisation that became the mainstay of the black-face minstrel show. The generally accepted version, which appears in Sigmund Spaeth's *A History of Popular Music in America* (Random House, New York), is that Rice, an actor, heard a black street entertainer hopping and skipping down the street, singing: 'Wheel about an' turn an' do jis so, An' ebry time I wheel about I jump Jim Crow.' Rice added some words of his own, put on a black face and some ragged clothes and introduced the song and character as a major part of his act (*c.* 1829). It was an immediate success. He took the act to England where he appears to have made a great impact. Philip Howe wrote in his diary on 4 August 1837: 'Rice, the celebrated Jim Crow . . . entertains nobility at their parties; the ladies pronounce his black face "the fairest of the fair" . . . and the wits of London have established the Crow Club in honor of the Yankee buffoon.' Thus this crude comic black figure, created for the entertainment of white audiences, provided the label for the race segregation laws.
D. H. Palmer, Macclesfield, Cheshire.

☐ THE song 'Jump Jim Crow' popularised the use of the name as a synonym for any black male. But the phrase has been dated back to 1730 when black people were first described as crows (*Dictionary of Eponyms*: Martin Manser).
Keith Cook, Manor Park, London E12.

☐ THE origins of the phrase in 18th-century plantation culture may have some connection to the legendary West African chieftain John Canoe (or Jim Kano), who is

celebrated to this day in the annual Junkanoo carnival in the Bahamas.
Martin Walker, Washington DC.

QUESTION: What would happen if, whilst cruising along the motorway at 80 mph, I move the gearstick into reverse and release the clutch?

☐ YOU very quickly reverse into the police car that is after you for speeding!
John Limrick, Enfield, Middlx.

☐ THERE are two methods of engaging and disengaging gears in a manually operated gearbox: the sliding spur, or 'crash' gear change; and the synchromesh gear change. The former method works by sliding one gear along a splined shaft until it engages fully with its mating gear, which then drives it at the ratio determined by the relative number of teeth on each gear. Engagement is only possible if both gears are stationary, or have the same peripheral velocity and rotate in the opposite direction to one another. The reverse gear, because it is normally engaged when the vehicle is stationary, is likely to be of the cheaper, sliding-spur type. Thus, with a vehicle travelling at 80 mph in a forward direction, it would be impossible to engage the reverse gear, since the relative gears would be rotating in the same direction. Attempting to engage reverse gear would only result in removal of particles of gear teeth, causing varying degrees of damage and accompanying excruciating noise, whilst the vehicle would continue, now out of drive, in the same direction; possibly slowing to the legal limit.
Brian Fowler, Great Alne, War.

☐ DRIVING an automatic on an ordinary road at around 50

mph, and thinking to move the gear selector level from 2 to Drive, I actually moved it from Drive to Reverse. There was a bang, a jolt, a screech, and the car was suddenly on the other side of the road and facing in the opposite direction. Fortunately there was no other traffic around and the gearbox and car were unaffected by the episode. I can't say the same for my passenger.

Pat Goss, Durham.

QUESTION: If I were to build a circular wall in space with a circumference of 372,000 miles, and then placed a powerful optical laser at the centre of the circle and rotated it at one revolution per second, would the speed of the laser's light dot across the wall be twice the speed of light? Or would the concept come to grief on some relativistic frame of reference?

☐ THIS does not violate the law that nothing can exceed the speed of light because the dot of light is not itself an object, but a series of photons hitting the wall that we interpret as a single entity. No single photon (light particle) is moving along the surface of the wall, so no single photon is travelling the circuit of the wall in one second. Rather, the situation is more like a cinema marquee with many light bulbs, but with only one lit at any given moment. Turning the bulbs on and off in staggered succession may give the impression of one light moving very quickly across the length of the marquee, but in fact nothing is moving at all. Similarly, nothing would be moving across the surface of the circular wall in space; there would only be a succession of photons hitting it, which we would interpret as a pattern of a moving dot.

Ronald L. Chrisley, School of Cognitive & Computing Sciences, University of Sussex.

QUESTION: How did the sausage-in-batter dish, 'Toad in the Hole' get its name?

□ THE name originates from the last century, when there was an upsurge in interest in archaeology and fossil hunting. This craze was fuelled by reports of live prehistoric animals being found encased in limestone, a toad being the most common animal alleged to have been discovered. This popular fascination even led to experiments involving live toads being placed in a hole and covered up with some suitable material.
Richard Bridgman, Wandsworth, London SW18.

□ THIS is a literal translation of the classic French dish known in the Dordogne as *Crapaud dans le Trou*. The dish was originally introduced to Britain by French prisoners during the Napoleonic Wars. In Britain the batter is made with flour whereas the French use only seasoned eggs and milk; and in France it is traditional to use herbs or spicy sausages rather than Britain's supermarket banger.
Simon Steele, London W1.

□ How did the sausage-in-batter dish *Crapaud dans le Trou* get its name? Is it similar in any way to that other classic French dish *Coq en Boule*?
Alastair Fraser, Bristol.

QUESTION: I once heard someone on radio refer to a pudding called Wet Nellie. Can any of your readers supply the recipe or a description?

□ WET NELLIES were flat cakes coated in syrup, and this would run down the pile of stacked cakes in the shop windows in Liverpool. Tommy Handley, the famous

wartime radio comedian of ITMA fame, said that as kids his contemporaries asked the shopkeeper for 'a ha'penny Wet Nellie, and can I have the one off the bottom please' – to gain maximum syrup saturation.
Peter Kenyon, Ponteland, Newcastle upon Tyne.

□ THE recipe is as follows: ½lb white breadcrumbs; 5 fl oz water; 2 teaspoons mixed spice; 4 oz chopped suet; 4 oz sugar. Soak the breadcrumbs in water for 30 minutes, add the spice, suet and sugar. Spoon the mixture into a greased, rectangular tin and bake for 1½ hours at gas mark 4 until firm. Serve hot or cold, cut into squares. This was originally made with crusts of bread, left over from bread sauce. It is said to originate from Lancashire. (Source: Boyd L., *British Cookery: A Complete Guide to Culinary Practice in the British Isles*.) I ate another version, which included apple, in an Amsterdam café some years ago: it was delicious.
Clive Vaisey, London SE11.

QUESTION: How many hours per week would each of us be working if work were shared out equitably, instead of some people being massively overworked and others unemployed?

□ ASSUMING that approximately 10 per cent of the workforce is out of work and that the remaining 90 per cent work on average 35 hours per week, then by simple arithmetic full employment would be achieved if we all chose to work 31.5 hours. Unfortunately, the skills of the unemployed do not match those in employment; the remainder of the workforce would not take very kindly to a 10 per cent cut in their real wages; and firms believe a return to full employment would drive wages up. On the other hand, the cost of financing unemployment through

the welfare state system would decrease. Reductions in taxes and National Insurance might increase the average take-home pay by, say, 5 per cent.
C. J. D. Roberts, West Hampstead, London NW6.

QUESTION: Why, on some roundabouts, is there a road passing through the centre with a gate at either end?

☐ SOME roundabouts, usually the larger ones, have a road across them to allow access and egress for emergency services or for maintenance of equipment on or under the roundabout. The gates, usually kept locked, are to prevent unauthorised entry. The best-known roundabout in the UK, at Hyde Park Corner in London, has a road across it which runs through Wellington Arch and may be used only by members of the royal family and the Household Cavalry travelling to and from the palace.
K. Delaney, Traffic and Road Safety Manager, RAC, London SW1.

☐ CONSTRUCTION of these roundabouts was once common in areas such as ours, where heavy engineering firms had to transport oversized loads. These loads were often long, and running them through roundabouts avoided damage to street furniture, such as lighting columns. It might be another indication of economic decline that such loads are far less common now.
David Walsh, Chair, Development & Transportation Committee, Cleveland County Council.

QUESTION: My father is deaf, but when he goes to the swimming pool there is something in the water that makes him hear. What is it?

☐ THE water makes him hear better. Water is a more dense fluid than air and as such transmits the sound vibrations more efficiently. When the head is immersed these vibrations are transmitted directly to the bones of the skull. This causes the bones of the middle ear to become excited to a greater degree than air-borne vibrations which affect the eardrum, and this increased vibration is sensed by the nerves situated in the cochlea, in the inner ear. In addition, when the head is raised from the water it is placed in a highly reverberant sound field. This causes the intensity of the sound to be raised.
Steven Payne, Frecheville, Sheffield.

QUESTION: For how long would a car have to be stationary to make it worth switching off the engine, thus saving fuel? (Assuming a typical car, properly tuned and at normal running temperature.)

☐ BRITISH PETROLEUM undertook research some years ago. Their answer was 90 seconds, give or take all the variables your readers will no doubt think of.
Frank Elliott, Bideford, Cornwall.

QUESTION: Mankind seems to be afflicted by a newly evolved disease every decade or so, Aids being but the latest example. Medical science has succeeded in controlling some, but few have been globally eradicated. Does this mean that the number of natural health threats is constantly growing?

☐ IT IS rather less the diseases which are evolving every decade so much as our ability to *detect* them emerging. The ancient Egyptians, Phoenicians and Greeks were familiar with diseases such as measles, smallpox and hepatitis, which gave distinctively overt skin surface symptoms; but the more subtle internal infections have probably been around for just as long, but grouped together under some more generalised heading. Thus *Legionella*, which 'emerged' in 1979, had been hidden behind the term pneumonia until the availability of antibiotics which cleared up the more common causes but revealed a further cause which did not respond to such treatments. Similarly, screening for the virus responsible for Hepatitis B failed to clear up all the cases of transfusion-associated hepatitis, and led to the characterisation of Hepatitis C in the late 1980s. HIV and Aids had probably been circulating in Africa in small remote pockets for a couple of thousand years until social changes brought about by 'westernisation' allowed the virus to emerge so devastatingly. Although smallpox was officially certified as eradicated in 1979, and many other species on this planet also made extinct by the activities of mankind, the microbial world has remained relatively unscathed. A dozen or more newly identified infections like toxic shock syndrome have come out of the woodwork since the early 1970s, several diseases like TB have become more active and vigorous, and yet others have become antibiotic-resistant. Other diseases are still awaiting the discovery of their causative agents.

Ian Shaw (virologist), Bromborough, Merseyside.

QUESTION: What is the oldest recorded joke? Who could claim to be the world's first inventor known by name?

☐ COULD it be when Eve said to Adam: 'Is that a serpent under your fig-leaf or are you pleased to see me?'
David Williams, Weeton, Lancs.

☐ I READ in some work on the Classics that the oldest joke is recorded in graffiti at Pompeii.
'How would you like your hair cut, sir?'
'In silence.'
Harold Smith, Bradford on Avon, Wilts.

☐ ONE contender can be found in book nine of Homer's *Odyssey*. The bloodthirsty Cyclops asks his prisoner, Odysseus, what his name is. 'My name is Nobody' (*Outis* in Greek) comes the answer. When, blinded in his one eye, Cyclops shrieks in pain, all he can say in explanation is: 'Nobody is killing me!'
Eleanor Nenbitt, Senior Research Fellow, University of Warwick, Institute of Education.

QUESTION: Where and when was punctuation first used? Who designed the question and exclamation marks?

☐ *THE BRITISH ENCYCLOPEDIA*, vol. 8 (1933) states: 'Our present system of punctuation came very gradually into use after the invention of printing – the Venetian printers the Manutii (of the late 15th and early 16th century) contributing materially to its development.'
Dorothy Platt, Eaton, Cheshire.

QUESTION: Where is Lydveldid Island? I saw a large plaque bearing this name on a building (complete with flag pole) in Park Street, London W1.

☐ ISLAND (pronounced 'eece-land') is what Icelanders call their beautiful (but misnamed) country, and what the questioner saw was the residence of His Excellency the

Ambassador of that nation. The words on the plaque mean
'The Republic of Iceland'. Incidentally, the third and final
letters of 'Lydveldid' are not actually Ds, but a character
peculiar to the Icelandic alphabet and pronounced like the
'the' in 'mother'.
Andrew Cauthery, Haslemere, Surrey.

**QUESTION: In Avignon the other week, people from all
over the world were singing '*Sur le pont d'Avignon*'
on the bridge itself. How did this ditty become so well
known?**

☐ APART from the fact that it is a catchy tune, nobody
knows. The bridge made its first appearance in 1613 in a
song '*La Péronnelle*' about a girl who had escaped to the
Dauphiné dressed as a page and was being brought back
forcibly *sur le pont d'Avignon* by her three brothers and
the *gens d'armes*. Later versions describe people passing
over and under the bridge, and there is even a French
Canadian '*Pont d'Avignon*' where three ladies drop their
combs which are then picked up by three Germans.
Nadine Laurence, Richmond, Surrey.

**QUESTION: I read somewhere that the first book of
the Bible was once called the Book of Swiving. If this
is true, when and why was it changed to Genesis?**

☐ THE quotation that the questioner recalls runs as follows: 'In the Scotch translation, Genesis is rendered the
Buke of Swiving' (*swiving* being the Old English term for
copulation). This phrase occurs in a collection of satirical
character studies by the English Restoration poet Samuel
Butler and is typical of Butler's use of overstatement
to ridicule what he saw as the coarse unspirituality of

Presbyterian (Scotch) religion. The same point is made at rather greater length in his epic satire *Hudibras*. For Butler, religious fanaticism, whether Puritan or Popish, inevitably drives away the true Christian message; and, in effect, reduces the Bible story to an unedifying collection of bonkings and battles.

Tom Hennell, Withington, Manchester.

QUESTION: I was taught in school that, on railway lines, there had to be a regular space between the lengths of rail to cope with expansion in hot weather. Nowadays, railway track is welded in seemingly endless lengths and does not appear to buckle. How so?

☐ ALL continuously welded rail is 'stretched' mechanically when it is installed. This 'stretching' is equivalent to the expansion caused by a ground temperature of 80°F. Furthermore, the assembly of sleepers and chairs is deeply ballasted to prevent lateral or longitudinal movement of the rails. Expansion of the rails now only takes place when the ground temperature is greater than 80°F, and typically this will be slight and is absorbed without buckling the track. Conversely when the ground temperature is freezing, the rails are in considerable tension. Occasionally in this situation a rail can break. This can have the effect of creating a gap of some inches in the running rails. Your correspondent may be interested to know that there are still many hundreds of passenger lines which have jointed track.

John France, Clifton, York.

QUESTION: When a fly is making its approach to land on a ceiling, does it fly upside down or does it flip over in the last micro-second before landing?

☐ THIS question was asked on the *Brains Trust* programme on the radio a few years ago when Commander Campbell, Dr C. E. M. Joad and Sir Malcolm Sargent treated it as a joke, but Professor Julian Huxley was quite angry that he didn't know what he thought he ought to have known. The following week, I believe, he returned to say that he had conducted experiments which showed that the fly flew closer to the ceiling until its first two legs could be put over its head to touch, and adhere to, the ceiling, bringing the rest of its body up to leave the creature on the ceiling and facing in the opposite direction.
V. Beilby, Fareham, Hants.

☐ THIS question was the subject of intensive study by an American convict. After many years of observation he said that, in the process of landing on the ceiling, flies always perform a half-upwards loop. To start flying again, they have to complete this loop. To prove it, the convict invented this way of catching flies: nearly fill a glass with soapy water, beat up a bit of a foamy head on the surface and raise the glass slowly from directly beneath the fly. Once the surface of the foam is about an inch and a half from the fly, it is doomed. In completing the interrupted loop, the fly cannot but dive into the foam.
Dulcie Kirby, Franschhoek, South Africa.

☐ PROFESSOR JOAD, in the *Brains Trust*, 1941, said: 'It all depends on what the fly had for lunch. Normally it lands on the ceiling by a loop-the-loop, but if it had too much to drink it does a roll.'
Peter Helsdon, Chelmsford, Essex.

QUESTION: Rock samples were brought back from the moon by the Apollo space missions in the late 1960s and early 1970s. Were they similar to rocks found on earth,

or were they totally different? And are any minerals on the moon worth exploiting?

☐ Moon rocks are all volcanic and are comparable with similar rocks on the earth, although there are slight but significant chemical differences, because the moon is a fossil world, unchanged for the past 3.8 thousand million years. This is the age of the youngest moon rocks, older than any existing earth rocks and therefore belonging to an early period of planetary evolution. On earth, rocks of this period have long ago been recycled by the processes of plate tectonics and weathering. Because of its smaller size the moon lacks these, having frozen into a static world nearly four thousand million years ago, while the larger earth has continued to sustain both internal and surface activity.
David Land, Edinburgh.

☐ In an article in *Scientific American* for July 1994 Professor G. Jeffrey Taylor, who chairs the committee that advises NASA on its missions, describes the outcome of studying the 382 kilograms of rock samples collected from the moon 25 years ago. This analysis supported the view that the moon originated from a glancing collision between the earth and another protoplanet four and a half thousand million years ago. The impact may be one of the factors that made the earth habitable, by speeding up its rotation time from perhaps a year to a day. The heat generated left the moon covered with a sea of molten rock and devoid of water. A more systematic collection covering more of the moon's surface could test the theory that the evolution of life on earth has been driven by mass extinctions, of 90 per cent or more of species and individuals living at the time, caused by impacts from smaller objects at intervals of tens of millions of years. Professor Taylor concludes: 'Only by continuing the legacy of Apollo can we hope to complete

our understanding of our place in the solar system.'
Professor Romaine Hervey, Wells, Somerset.

QUESTION: Since moths are so attracted by light, why don't they come out in the daytime?

☐ THEY DO! The males (more expendable than the females) of the Emperor Moth – *Saturnia pavonia* (Linnaeus) – zigzag around heathland on sunny afternoons in May, looking for females resting in blackthorn or heather. Eggars like afternoon flights and Burnets can be found sunning themselves on various plants; Hawkmoths and Noctuids prefer evenings. But almost all the 2,000 or so British species do fly at night as well. All moth species have evolved 'awareness' of the day's cycle and their behaviour patterns are triggered by dawn and dusk. Each species has its own rhythm of activity but they are, in general, adapted to the less dry conditions of night-time. Many moths are attracted to light at the near-ultraviolet end of the spectrum; many flowers have UV patterns on the petals. Moths appear attracted to artificial lights as a side effect of an attempt to travel in a straight line. (They do this to aid their search for food-plants or mates.) The compound eye of the moth is adapted to detect any change of angle of a distant point light source. For millions of years, this light source can only have been the moon or the sun, and keeping it at the same angle while flying ensured that the moth didn't waste energy flying in circles. Unfortunately, keeping a nearby artificial light at a constant angle means that the moth flies towards the light on a logarithmic spiral.
Copland Smith, Chorlton-cum-Hardy, Manchester.

QUESTION: I learnt from Woody Allen's *Broadway*

Danny Rose that the American expression 'to be a beard' is the equivalent of our expression 'to play gooseberry'. How did this use of these terms come about?

☐ DANNY ROSE was not a 'gooseberry'. A gooseberry is an unwelcome or uninvited third party. Danny Rose was the beard; he was invited specifically to mislead, to distract attention from the real liaison that was taking place. It is impossible to be certain of the origins of this phrase but I assume that it derives from the fact that a beard is the easiest item of disguise or deception.
Michael Glickman, London NW5.

☐ 'TO BE a beard' is gay slang referring to a woman who, wittingly or unwittingly, appears as a gay man's girlfriend/date/partner in order for him to pass as straight. She gives him, to the straight world, virility; the beard being the obvious symbol to represent such an arrangement.
Richard Krupp, Maida Vale, London W9.

QUESTION: We are often told that the UK's economy has been in relative decline for decades. How do we now rate internationally and should the UK still be a member of G7?

☐ VARIOUS national audit figures show the UK's poor, almost catastrophic, position in relation to other advanced economies. In 1990, Britain's output per head was £12,000, well behind Luxemburg (£21,600) and, of EC members, ahead of only Spain, Ireland, Greece and Portugal. On these grounds we have a very weak claim to a seat at the table of advanced economies. However, the City of London is one of the chief operators in the game of currency speculation; however harmful this may be in

the long run, the UK can, on this ground alone, claim to be in on the wheeling and dealing of G7 conferences, though I suspect that our views are of little weight.
Bernard Keeffe, London SE23.

QUESTION: Seventy years ago I learnt to play what was described as 'an American organ' in my uncle's smallish living room. Do such instruments still exist and what can you tell me about them?

☐ YES, these organs still exist, but are very hard to find. I played a lovely American organ some 60 years ago. I actually saw one recently, a 'Malcolm Organ' by John Murdoch & Co. Ltd of London. The American organ is a kind of harmonium. It is played in much the same way; the blowing is much easier and does not need any special study in using the treadles. Owing to differences in the thickness and the shape of the reeds, the tone is not so powerful as that of the harmonium, but is more organ-like. The organ has 10 to 13 stops and seven sets or more of reeds with two knee swells – crescendo and diminuendo being produced by the knees of the player bending outwards. Some organs have a single set of reeds, large ones have many.
David Norris, Dover, Kent.

☐ WE HAVE one in our dining room. It has on it 'Needham, New York', and also notifies one where it might be bought: 'Sole North Devon Agents, O. Nicklin & Sons'. An American organ is a metal reed organ, rather like a piano, but having a keyboard of only about five octaves (in common with most types of organ) rather than a piano's 85 keys. The sound of an American organ is produced by air passing through a rectangular orifice (whose width is only a fraction of an inch) which has a metal reed attached at one end to the metal base plate. For each note there are two reeds so that the quality of sound may be varied. The reed vibrates and produces a note corresponding to its natural frequency (dependent upon its length). The air to produce the sound is moved by means of a pump (connected to foot pedals) which evacuates air from a large bag in the base of the instrument. The American organ is very similar to an harmonium. The American organ pumps air *out* of the bag, and the harmonium pumps air (as you pedal) *into* the bag, then out via the reeds. The American organ is reckoned to be a bit more responsive to the keyboard than the harmonium but neither can really compete with the pipe organ for tone and volume, particularly in the higher ranges. Reed organs of either type were common in places of worship many years ago, and those from chapels tend to be truncated (so that the organist could see over the top). Organs intended for home use often had ornate tops with rococo decoration and mirrors and were intended to be positioned against the wall.

Dave Clark, Taunton, Somerset.

QUESTION: TV documentaries on the moon-landings have compared today's computer technology with that available to NASA a quarter of a century ago. It has been claimed that a modern lap-top is as powerful as the whole of Apollo's mission control. Can anyone give definitive figures?

☐ THE first mainframe computer I worked on was an Elliott 4120. It had 32k words of memory (we didn't have bytes in those days). One word was 24 bits long and held four 6-bit characters, so I suppose it could be taken as 4 bytes to the word. This made the computer's total memory 128k bytes. My present 486-based PC has

4 megabytes of RAM; 32 times as much. Mass storage on the 4120 was magnetic tape. Disk drives did exist but we didn't have one. Our usual reel of tape was 1,200 feet long and information was stored at 200 bits to the inch. At eight bits to one byte, 1,200 feet of tape would hold 360,000 bytes. This is roughly equal to 350k bytes; my PC has diskettes holding 1.44 megabytes. Not only that, the magnetic tapes were about 9 inches in diameter, compared with 3.5 inches for the diskettes. If that wasn't enough, the magnetic tapes were serial devices (that is, if the data to be read was at the end of the tape, it was necessary to read right through to find it); the diskettes have almost instantaneous access to any part of the data. Speed of operation of the PC is greater by a factor of thousands; the mainframe occupied a room 25 feet by 10 feet while the PC sits on a desk; the mainframe cost £90,000 at 1967 prices while the PC cost about £1,500 at 1994 prices. Add to that the incredible range of cheap software and the modern PC has computing power only dreamed of in 1967.

Dudley Turner, Westerham, Kent.

QUESTION: Where can I buy a Tony Blair Coronation Mug?

☐ I EXPECT there will be a special offer in the *Sun* or *The Times* coming along any time now.
George Barrow, London N4.

☐ TRY the Parliamentary Labour Party: there are plenty of mugs there who voted for him.
Mike McIlroy, Hoghton, Preston, Lancs.

☐ YOU'LL be lucky to find one; Tony Blair has sold out.
Helen Wilson, Balsall Heath, Birmingham.

QUESTION: Are we still evolving or is this as good as we get?

□ THE advent of genetic engineering will allow us to fast-forward the rate of evolution and shape our progeny according to our whims. Regardless of whether this is desirable, it is uncontrollable and only a matter of time before this technology transforms humanity. Some scientists such as Hans Moravec go even further, and suggest that a 'genetic takeover' is under way, where artificial computerised life-forms will start to evolve faster than their organic counterparts. Aided by us and unfettered by biological constraints, these programs will develop intelligence in advance of our own. Rather than being wiped out by our creations, we will be able to copy our brain patterns on to computers and transcend our bodies, 'becoming' these cybernetic super-beings.
Chris Mungall, Edinburgh.

□ NO ANSWER is possible. Evolution is a classic example of a chaotic process – with a touch of catastrophe theory thrown in. Each micro-step is rational, but the future state is unpredictable from any knowledge we can attain of the present state. We can, of course, speculate. We could say that man is a recent arrival on the scene, embodying exciting new developments, with lots of potential. He lacks features that species that have been around for significant evolutionary time have – for example the ability to control his population – but these deficiencies may be balanced by his ability to use intelligent behaviour to solve physiological problems in a fraction of the time biological adaptation would take. On the other hand, the current view is that evolution proceeds in surges that follow mass extinctions caused by such events as comets hitting the earth. It is not too difficult to imagine that the next mass extinction may be due to human action and will

include man. That would not actually be unprecedented.
When algae discovered photosynthesis and filled the
earth's atmosphere with oxygen, pre-existing anaerobic
organisms, had they been articulate, must have described
this as a dreadful catastrophe, and they ceased to be the
dominant life forms. We, however, looking back, see the
event as 'good'. There seems to be a principle at work,
which we do not understand, that causes physical and
biological evolution to proceed toward greater complexity
and in some sense 'forward'. (St Paul had the insight
that 'all things are moving toward perfection'.) I think
our knowledge of the earth's history justifies optimism,
whatever the future of our particular species.
Professor Romaine Hervey, Wells, Somerset.

☐ IF THERE were an ice age next week, with massive crop
failures, famines and a general 'collapse of civilisation',
then you can be certain that evolutionary pressures would
once again come to bear. People more able to tolerate the
cold (large and fat?) would be more likely to survive to
breeding age; very hairy men (and women), who might
be sexually unattractive now, would quickly establish a
foothold in the gene pool.
David Gibson, Leeds.

**QUESTION: Do diet drinks which contain no sugar
still cause dental decay?**

☐ DIET colas are highly acidic – the pH of Diet Coke is
2.89. A few years ago, when my children were small, we put
one of their teeth in a glass of diet cola. In the morning the
tooth had dissolved. Cola drinks contain a large amount of
phosphate and on Radio Four's *Food Programme* in 1993
an eminent US professor stated that these drinks may
be responsible for osteoporosis in humans because they

replace bone calcium. Diet cola is also a better spermicide than old 'Classic', 'New' and 'Caffeine Free'.
John McGarry, Barnstaple, N. Devon.

□ DIET drinks do not usually contain sugar, and so cannot cause dental decay. However, soft drinks, especially carbonated ones, are generally acidic and can cause dental erosion. This is a progressive loss of enamel and dentine resulting from chemical attack. Some 'no added sugar' drinks contain hidden sugars such as fructose and these can cause decay, so it is important to check the label. The advice of the dental profession is to keep consumption of all soft drinks, including sugar-free varieties, to a reasonable level and preferably to meal times. The more often you consume sugary foods and drinks, the higher the number of attacks to the tooth enamel and the more damage is done.
Sara Morris, British Dental Association, London W1.

□ THE phosphoric acid which rots teeth is largely neutralised by saliva. In the few studies done, the main problem appears to be cavities in the front teeth as the cola washes past them into the mouth. Putting teeth in glasses of Coke might scare children, but it is hardly a scientific experiment. The studies suggest that colas should be drunk with a straw so that the cola misses the front teeth. Incidentally, orange juice is just as acidic as cola.
Mark Lee, Sheffield.

QUESTION: Was Asclepius, the ancient Greek physician said to appear in his patients' dreams and administer healing (often by performing 'surgery'), man, myth, or both? And what is the explanation for the numerous 'offerings' (in the form of inscriptions

**on tablets or terracotta models of the healed body part
or organ) supposedly left by grateful patients?**

☐ Asclepius was a myth, said to be the progeny of
Apollo, a god, and of Coronis, a mortal woman. Apollo's
sister Artemis killed the pregnant Coronis but Asclepius
was saved by post-mortem Caesarean section. Asclepius
became a great healer. After he had been struck dead
by Zeus he was resurrected as a god. His tale inspired
Greek healers for centuries. The healing temples originated
about the 6th century BC. Many healing techniques were
used including magic, drugs and surgery. One sleeping
method was preceded by elaborate ritual and sacrifices.
Grateful patients then made offerings to the temple of
terracotta. These were models of the part which had been
healed, and common examples include limbs, breasts,
ears and genitals. The magic was effective for the same
reason that almost any therapeutic procedure, orthodox or
unorthodox, tends to help, especially if the patient has faith
in the treatment. There is a placebo effect, a well recognised
psycho-somatic phenomenon which should not be decried.
In addition, time cures many diseases. This explains many
cures claimed by healers of all kinds down the ages.
Dr Michael L. Cox, Higham on the Hill, War.

☐ Asclepius may have been a myth, but the Egyptian
Imhotep, who was identified with Asclepius, was definitely
historical. Imhotep is recorded as holding the high offices
of chief executive and master sculptor during the reign of
King Zoser of the 3rd Dynasty (*c.* 2650 BC). It is likely that
he was the architect of the king's tomb, the Step Pyramid
at Saggara – the first large building in the world to be
built entirely of stone. After his death he was deified, and
during the Graeco-Roman period (*c.* 332 BC – AD 395)
he was worshipped as a god in cult centres and temples
throughout Egypt. Imhotep's posthumous reputation as

a healer at a time of Greek rule over Egypt led to the identification with Greek Asclepius.

Dr Piotr Bienkowski, Curator of Egyptian and Near Eastern Antiquities, Liverpool Museum.

QUESTION: Is there any sport which was invented by a woman?

☐ COURTSHIP. This is a well-known sport in which a man chases a woman until she catches him.
Len Clarke, Uxbridge, Middlx.

☐ I RECALL reading that overarm bowling was invented by a woman whose voluminous skirts interfered with an underarm action.
E. Hunter, London SE4.

☐ ACCORDING to Chinese legends, a form of martial art from southern China was said to have been invented by a nun named Ng Mui. She had seen how martial arts had been adapted to the male physique and temperament, and decided that martial arts could also be adapted to women. The combination of short, fast and powerful offensive hand techniques with a soft and effective defence made this extremely useful. Ng Mui met a young girl who was being attacked by village men, the story goes. Ng Mui decided to teach the girl, Wing Chun, her martial art so that she could defend herself. Wing Chun Kung Fu has been practised by millions of people around the world, including the late Bruce Lee.
K. W. Pang, Leatherhead, Surrey.

☐ NETBALL was invented in 1895 at the Osterberge College of Physical Education, Dartford. This was an all-female establishment and one of its students also designed the

gymslip which became the uniform for schoolgirls and sportswomen.
Marion Tofts, Dartford, Kent.

QUESTION: Why do some single malt Scotch whiskies go slightly cloudy when water is added whereas blended whiskies never do?

☐ I PRESUME this is a special effect engineered by the distillers to try to discourage you from adulterating your single malt with water. Blended whiskies exist for the purpose of mixing them with other substances of varying noxiousness; the quality of the whisky is not seriously impaired by this practice. Single malts should be drunk straight; if you don't like whisky enough to do this, then stick to the other stuff.
Richard A'Brook, Carnoustie, Angus.

☐ THE cloudiness will be due to the release of dissolved substances from solution in the alcohol. Presumably malt whisky has a higher concentration of ethyl alcohol, therefore stronger than blended whiskies, which have already been diluted during the blending process. Thus the precipitation will have taken place before purchase, i.e. during the blending process.
B. P. Gay, Orpington, Kent.

☐ MESSRS A'BROOK AND GAY are misinformed. On a visit to a famous highland distillery, I was informed that the only thing to mix with any whisky, whether blended or malt, is water. One hundred per cent proof whisky is 50 per cent spirit and 50 per cent water, so how can there be harm in adding more water? The Scottish habit of drinking it neat in one gulp is connected with machismo, not connoisseurship.
John Bowler, Painswick, Glos.

QUESTION: How does a 'Switch' payment work? What safeguards are there to prevent error? I have recently had a single purchase debited seven times.

☐ I AM concerned to hear of this problem. It is the first incident of this kind I have heard. On reaching the point of sale, the Switch cardholder offers their card to the cashier who 'swipes' it through an electronic terminal and a receipt is produced for signature. The card details and amount are captured in the terminal and later transferred electronically to the retailer's bank. This information is collated, the retailer's account credited and the cardholder's bank presented with the information for debiting – which happens a day or two after the purchase. There are 13 million Switch cardholders who will undertake over 400 million purchases worth £11 billion this year alone. The overwhelming number of transactions are carried out without a hitch. However, in common with any system that processes over 1 million transactions every day, the occasional problem can occur.
Nigel Turner, Head of Marketing, Switch Card Services Ltd, London EC2.

☐ NIGEL TURNER'S answer is accurate, but incomplete. When a Switch card is used in a shop, it is indeed swiped through a magnetic stripe reader, and a signed receipt produced to record the cardholder's authorisation of the transaction. However, Mr Turner does not mention that Switch cards can also be used over the telephone. In this case the purchaser need only quote the card number and expiry date, whereupon his bank account is immediately debited. There is no other authentication or check that the use is authorised by the cardholder, so the opportunity for fraud is obvious. Although the mechanism seems similar to a telephone credit-card transaction, there are two important differences: a credit-card user can examine his statement and query transactions before he has to pay for them, whereas Switch transactions are immediately debited from the holder's account; and users of credit cards, unlike Switch cards, have some legal protection under the Consumer Credit Act. I've told my bank that I wish to withdraw my consent to telephone Switch transactions. They tell me that they can't do this, and in any case no one else has ever expressed concern. Perhaps this is because so few realise that Switch cards can be used in this way?

Andrew Watson, Cambridge.

□ I THINK Mr Turner's defence of Switch could have been more succinct:

Switch
Goes without a hitch
Except for the occasional glitch.

Andrew Belsey, Cardiff.

QUESTION: The Cubist paintings of Picasso and Braque contain a variety of musical instruments. As well as the familiar guitars, clarinets, violins, mandolins, a piano and even a metronome can be identified. Does anyone know what other music the Cubists either played or heard, and how far did their music inspire their unprecedented inventions?

□ THE work of Picasso also includes pan-pipes, flute, tambourine, balalaika, the Hurdy Gurdy and concertina as well as sheet music. He played guitar a little. Other musical connections include his marriage to a ballet dancer, Olga, and in 1909 he designed costumes and sets for *The Three-Cornered Hat* and other ballets. And in *Guernica* he includes an electric bell. Braque played concertina and had in his studio a mandolin, a small violin, an African harp and his concertina. In 1937–9 Braque produced a series of drawings and paintings including *Le Pianiste*, showing a woman playing an upright piano, and later a woman playing a mandolin. He may have played the organ in the church near his holiday home in Varengeville in Normandy. They both frequented the Lapin Agile in Paris and heard the guitar playing of its owner, Frede. Their use of musical instruments was as objects which could be visually disassembled and reorganised against their background; and of course they used fruit, furniture, bottles and the human figure in the same way.

John Maher, Peckham, London SE15.

QUESTION: Capgras' syndrome is a mental disorder where sufferers believe that someone they know has been replaced by an identical imposter. What tests do psychologists make to prove or disprove whether a substitution has been made?

□ CAPGRAS' syndrome is usually seen as part of a psychotic illness such as schizophrenia. As such, it is usually treated by psychiatrists, who are medically trained, as opposed to psychologists. The belief concerned is a delusional idea. A delusion is defined as a belief that is held on inadequate grounds and is not affected by rational argument or evidence to the contrary. Thus the 'test' of Capgras' syndrome is for the psychiatrist to examine the patient's mental state to ascertain the grounds upon which his or her belief is based. If these appear in commonsense terms to be inadequate, the diagnosis can be tentatively made. It is not the belief itself that is usually a problem, but the degree of emotion with which it is held and the actions the patient takes to bring him/her into the remit of psychiatric care. Also the reasons given are usually too bizarre to be credible.

Dr Danny Allen, Senior Registrar in Psychiatry, Frenchay Healthcare Trust, Bristol.

QUESTION: Weather forecasts often refer to 'showers or longer periods of rain'. How long does a shower have to last before it can more correctly be described as a period of rain?

☐ AS YOU nip round the corner to collect your *Guardian* it starts to rain and you decide not to go back for your car. If, as you get back, it stops raining and you're only a bit damp – that's been a shower. If you've guessed wrong and get back soaked – that's rain.

A. I. Pottinger, Edgbaston, Birmingham.

☐ STRICTLY speaking, showers only fall from unstable clouds such as cumulo-nimbus. These usually cover a relatively small horizontal area, hence tend to move on after a short time. A prolonged shower lasts longer than about half an hour, and sometimes showers from adjacent storm cells merge together to give longer periods of rain – longer than about an hour.

Barry Parker, Met Office, Bracknell, Berks.

QUESTION: Dragons have been described in art and myth for thousands of years. Dragons and certain dinosaurs are remarkably similar in appearance. Is this just coincidence?

□ THE only feature dragons and dinosaurs have in common is their monstrosity. Dinosaurs did exist, while dragons were fearful creatures peopling fables and legends. Melville states in *Moby Dick* that dragons are in fact whales. He is clearly biased, but I nevertheless think it very possible. Human imagination has led to great inventions and it doesn't take much to turn a whale into a dragon. Whales, because of their great dimensions, are an ideal start to express the human sense of immensity and our fears of the unknown. Dragons are, however, better candidates to embody such feelings because of their repellent appearance and their fantastic and unpredictable character.
Marta Fumagalli, Edinburgh.

□ PERHAPS not. The Chinese are particularly devoted to dragons, and have been for millennia. And where is one of the richest dinosaur graveyards? China. So might not the very concept of dragons have come from exposed fossils of large dinosaurs? After all, Britain's ammonite fossils were originally thought to be the remains of coiled snakes of various sizes, and belemnites were thought to have been formed in the soil by lightning.
Len Clarke, Uxbridge, Middlx.

□ DRAGONS are descended from serpents, not from dinosaurs. The early tribal Celts depicted snakes with rams' horns as well as with wings. The early Greek symbol of the winged serpent, associated with Hippocrates and later with Hermes or Mercury as his caduceus, is now universally recognised as a symbol for medicine. Dragon breath is a metaphor for snake venom, which often produces hallucinatory as well as fatal effects. In Eastern mythologies, serpents, often with mysterious powers, guard treasure hoards. In the West, the same function is performed by dragons. In both cases, the creatures may represent the physical and spiritual barriers which initiates must overcome in order to attain the treasure of arcane or esoteric knowledge. Dragons also lay eggs and have forked tongues.

John King, Cornwall, Connecticut.

QUESTION: Who, or what, are Marjorie Daw and Johnny, as in 'See-saw, Marjorie Daw, Johnny shall have a new master . . .'? And what is the origin of this children's rhyme?

☐ PETER AND IONA OPIE in *The Oxford Dictionary of Nursery Rhymes* suggest that the song may have been sung by sawyers to keep to the rhythm of the two-handled saw. This would also help to explain the line 'Jacky must have but a penny a day, because he can't work any faster'. Any youngsters playing nearby – perhaps using a sawyer's plank as a see-saw – could easily have picked up the song. Margery was a very common name among the rural poor in 18th- and 19th-century England. Daw is given in the *OED* as 'a lazy person, sluggard'. Whilst 'daw' was also used in Scotland to denote 'an untidy woman, slut, slattern', early variants of the see-saw song were generally collected in England. Certainly the social setting is crucial, though in this case we don't really know what that was! Another difficulty is that songs are often altered or interpreted according to contemporary views, and original intentions become obscured. Given this, it is difficult to say whether the song was based on a specific person or not.

Brian Holmshaw, English Folk Dance and Song Society, London NW1.

☐ 'SEE-SAW' as chanted by children has an equivalent among French children, *'ci-seaux'* ('scissors'). The

rhyme could have started as a French song which, in the French–English bilingual community of Canadian lumberjacks, was transposed (rather than translated) into English. The first line would have been: *'Ci-seaux, ma chérie dort'* ('my darling is asleep . . .').
Jenny Heimerdinger, Harefield, Middlx.

QUESTION: If an actor can use a stuntman in films, what happens in the case of children? Is there such a thing as a 'stunt-child'?

☐ The second of the Indiana Jones films featured a child as one of the three main characters. While the film was being made in Britain, I stayed at the Royal Lancaster Hotel in London and was introduced to another guest who was the child actor's stunt double. It was a long time ago, but I think he was American and was about 4 feet tall so his head was on a level with my chest.
Ken Clayton, Tamworth, Staffs.

☐ A local man, Joe Fox, was the 16-year-old stand-in for the 12-year-old actor who portrayed the young Pip in the 1948 film of *Great Expectations*. In the early sequences of the film, Pip is to be seen running from the graveyard across ploughed fields. The 'field' was in a studio – the furrows were of wood, covered with earth. The boy actor might have sprained his ankle, so Mr Fox ran for him. The following year Mr Fox was in the play *No Room at the Inn* in which, as one of the mistreated evacuees, he was taught to withstand scratchings and punchings.
E. F. Evans, Bradford on Avon, Wilts.

QUESTION: What is the correct verb to describe the movement of a submarine?

☐ SUBMARINES are boats. Boats sail. Submarines do also dive but forward motion can only be sailing, which is the verb describing boats' forward motion regardless of the method of propulsion. I don't like the description, but I feel I can claim to be an expert after spending 24 years training submariners at RN College Greenwich.
B. P. Gay, Orpington, Kent.

QUESTION: Was there ever really a phrase-book containing the sentence: 'My postilion has been struck by lightning?'

☐ MANY years ago I bought a second-hand Baedekker of, I think, 1882. Unhappily the book has gone missing but, as I recall, the full phrase was something like: 'Driver – stop the coach! The postilion has been struck by lightning.' Another phrase which sticks in my memory was in the section on crossing frontiers: 'Do not keep me waiting, my good man! Do you not realize that I am the holder of Her Britannic Majesty's passport?'
Peter James, East Malling, Kent.

☐ A COLLEAGUE of mine has just left for Vietnam armed with a copy of *How to Speak Vietnamese*, which was originally a phrase book for missionaries in past centuries. In the section at the railway station you can learn '*Có vé cho chó không?*' ('Are there tickets for dogs?')
Martin Nugent, Augsburg, Germany.

QUESTION: I have a photograph of an inverted rainbow, formed in the sky in the usual way: it just curves the 'wrong' way. The sun was in its customary position, and there was no other extraordinary event that anyone noticed. What could have produced this?

☐ RAINBOWS are formed from the prismatic effect of light passing through a fine water spray – most commonly, rain. You can see little rainbows in swimming pools or when using a hose or sprinkler in the garden, and these are seen as full circles. At sea level, one can only see a large rainbow's upper half, but in an aircraft one can see the whole circle. I suspect your photograph shows the bottom of a rainbow taken from an aircraft. Rainbows are, however, not circles, but nests of spherical sections; wherever the rainbow is viewed from, it always appears as a circle and never as an ellipse.
Jasper Smith, Oxford.

☐ THE inverted rainbow may have been the third rainbow. The first two rainbows, one outside the other, can often be observed. The third rainbow, however, is not only fainter, but it appears as a circle around the sun and therefore must compete with the sun's far greater light output. To view the first two rainbows, one stands with one's back to the sun so this problem does not arise.
J. B. Reade, Department of Maths, Manchester University.

☐ TO PRODUCE a rainbow effect where there is no rainbow, a 'rainbow filter' is placed over the camera lens; if put on upside down, the rainbow will appear upside down on the photograph.
Steve Turvey, Windermere, Cumbria.

☐ THIS is possible if the viewer, with his back to the sun, also has a reflecting surface, such as a sheet of calm (or very nearly calm) water behind him or her. The reflection of the sun from this surface can also produce a rainbow, with its centre placed as if the sun was below the horizon. A full circle could be produced under these circumstances,

and what the questioner has probably seen is a part circle comprising the lower half of the rainbow.
Malcolm Brooks, Met Office, Bracknell, Berks.

QUESTION: What exactly is or was a tantalus? I believe it was some sort of Victorian cabinet for bottles of booze, but how did it differ from any other drinks cabinet?

☐ A TANTALUS is a wooden-based container, easily held in the hand, which partly covered three (or sometimes two) cut-glass decanters for spirits. The wooden front, 2 or 3 inches high, is locked with a key. The hinged front drops forward when unlocked, and the decanters will then slide out. Locking the tantalus ensured that household staff did not drink the spirits, but the beautiful decanters could still be displayed. Often the finest wood was used. Brass overlay, sometimes with a family crest, enhanced the tantalus. The word tantalus comes from the Greek mythological character Tantalus, whose punishment was to be up to his chin in water which always receded when he attempted to drink it (hence the word *tantalise*). Smaller versions of the tantalus with elegant perfume bottles instead of the decanters are more rare.
Ruth Lewis, Sheffield.

QUESTION: Why do women's jackets never have inside pockets, and why are the outside pockets almost invariably sealed?

☐ MEN'S formal clothing is traditionally cut looser than women's – thus allowing pocket room. It is also made from heavier fabrics, preserving an even line because the bulge

of pockets is absorbed by the lining. The male jacket is cut to a more 'tubular' shape, falling from the width of the shoulders. Thus the lower reaches of the jacket sit looser and free over the waist – which is little narrower than the hips, in young men at least – allowing free space around the stomach and hips where pockets may fit. Women's jackets are usually cut to an 'hourglass' shape, with a curved dart to fit to the breast, and with narrower shoulders – hence the option of padding. Traditional pockets fall just below the breasts and across the hip bones. Anything bulky in them will push the hems and lapels grossly out of line, so the pocket flaps are 'visual punctuation' only. Thus the continuing necessity of the handbag, even with power-dressing suits.
Tony Clarke, Ely, Cambs.

☐ HAVING found it hard to buy my five-year-old daughter clothes with pockets, I concluded that girls are discouraged from carrying around marbles, matchboxes with spiders, money, etc. as training for adult life. Women's clothes are often pocketless to encourage them to hand over keys, money, credit cards, etc. – and therefore control – to the pockets of a male partner.
Duncan Cruickshank, Kingsdown, Wilts.

QUESTION: Why do the British pronounce lieutenant as 'leftenant'?

☐ ACCORDING to *The Shorter Oxford Dictionary*, the Old French labial glide at the end of the first syllable was heard by English ears as a 'v' or an 'f'. This could only apply with a compound word so that *lieu* as a word on its own would have been heard as 'lew'. It appears, moreover, that there was a rarer Old French form '*leuf*' which might give rise to the Scottish form 'lufftenand'.
John Jeffries, Oadby, Leics.

☐ WHEN I was a national serviceman in the senior service, I was informed that the preferred pronunciation for the rank of the toff on the bridge with two stripes on his sleeve was 'lettenant'. That was the way it was and had been since Nelson held the rank. Given that the Royal Navy had its own pronunciation for many things, like 'tayckle' for 'tackle' and 'forrard' for 'forward', this struck me as entirely reasonable. Trouble is, I observe that many sailors today do not seem to have been given the same advice and follow the curious habit of the land-locked forces of throwing in an unnecessary 'f'.

John Farrand, Kettleshulme, Cheshire.

QUESTION: What is the universe expanding into?

☐ THE simple answer is 'itself'. The universe is all there is, it has *no outside*. This is not the same as saying 'there is nothing outside' since that requires a boundary and the universe is boundless. The commonest metaphor used to try to visualise this is the child's balloon. The rubber of an inflating balloon expands, every point on it gets further from every other. Yet to a two-dimensional population living in its surface their world is not expanding *into* anything; it is mysteriously getting bigger. Of course, with this analogy of the universe, the big bang comes at the wrong end!

Patrick O'Neill, Eastleigh, Hants.

☐ IT IS not a vacuum, since that is inside the universe and is traversed by electrical, magnetic and gravitational fields. So one could describe the space beyond the boundary of the universe as nothing – a lack of anything, except, perhaps, thought of conscious beings. Matter expanding into 'nothing' at the boundary of the universe will have a negative electrical charge because this is repelled by

radiation pressure and will accelerate much more than relatively heavy matter with positive charges. This produces an increasing potential gradient, and eventually immense electrical discharges form huge jets of positively charged matter which condense to form the strings of galaxies we can now observe with our sophisticated telescopes and even binoculars. Most of the current 'mysteries' of astronomy can be explained without postulating bizarre ideas about so-called black holes and cosmic strings.
Eric Crew, Broxbourne, Herts.

QUESTION: Are humans the only animal species to have pudding?

☐ IMMEDIATELY after his main meal, my Jack Russell terrier goes to his biscuit bowl and consumes three or four of his dog biscuits. They are always there for him, but the only time he ever eats them is after his main meal. As yet he has not developed the sophisticated human habit of having custard with his pudding.
Ruth Harvey, Pontefract, W. Yorks.

☐ I ONCE watched a hedgehog and a slug drinking from a bowl of milk. When the hedgehog finished the milk it ate the slug.
John Malcolmson, Sheffield.

QUESTION: Has the course of events ever been changed significantly as a result of a letter written to, and published by, a national newspaper?

☐ IN MARCH 1918 when the Germans launched their great

attack in France, the Prime Minister Lloyd George stated in
Parliament that the British Army in France was stronger
in January 1918 than it had been 12 months earlier.
On 7 May there appeared in *The Times* and the *Daily
Telegraph* a letter from General Maurice, who had been
Director of Military Operations at the War Office, stating
that the Prime Minister had lied. The letter raised issues
wider than the Prime Minister's veracity. Behind it lay
the whole question of war strategy and the clash between
Lloyd George and Haig. At the time the German offensive
was still making formidable progress. Asquith challenged
the Government in what was, in effect, a vote of censure.
In the event the Government won by 293 votes to 106
but the Liberals divided, 71 for Lloyd George and 98
for Asquith. The Maurice letter and subsequent debate
had two consequences: the military were not again able
to challenge the Prime Minister in the conduct of the
war; and the Liberal Party never recovered from this
split. Those who supported Asquith were denied Lloyd
George's endorsement (the 'coupon') and most of them
lost their seats in the December 1918 election.
J. Owain Jones, Mold, Clwyd.

☐ ON 15 July 1944 *The Times* published a letter from Lady
Allen of Hurtwood drawing attention to the conditions
suffered by many children living in local authority
institutional care or that provided by voluntary agencies
which were 'repressive . . . generations out of date and
unworthy of our traditional care of children'. She went on
to say: 'Many who are orphaned, destitute or neglected still
live under the chilly stigma of "charity".' She criticised
having staff who were 'for the most part overworked,
underpaid and untrained' and the lack of recognised
training and adequate inspection and supervision. She
ended by calling for a public enquiry. A stream of letters
followed in her support, which the editor of *The Times*

twice sought to close and which at that time constituted the correspondence record in that newspaper. Six months later Lady Allen made her case again in a pamphlet, *Whose Children?* A few days after its publication the campaign was bolstered when the inquest into the death of 13-year-old Denis O'Neill, who had died at the hands of his foster father, having been boarded out in a remote farm in Shropshire by his local authority, was widely reported in the press. This agitation – largely prompted by that first letter – was responsible for the Government establishing the Curtis Committee in 1945 to investigate the care of children 'deprived of normal home life with their own families and relatives'. It reported in 1946 and led directly to the creation, under the Children Act 1948, of children's departments. The departments, until they were subsumed by the new social services departments in 1971, completely transformed for the better the face of official child care in England and Wales.

Terry Philpot, Oxted, Surrey.

QUESTION: Slavomir Rawicz, a Polish Army officer, wrote *The Long Walk* (Constable, 1956), telling of his escape from a Russian prison camp in Siberia in 1941 and how he walked with six companions to India. Is anything known about his later life, or his companions, especially the mysterious American Mr Smith?

☐ I AM now retired and living in the Midlands. After leaving India I spent some time with the Polish Forces in the Middle East, coming to England to join the Polish wing of the British Air Force. When the second world war was over I stayed in England and married an English woman from the Midlands. I had five children, two sons, three daughters, 11 grandchildren and a great-granddaughter. I was for some years involved with the Design and Building

Centre, and then with Trent Polytechnic, as it was then. I took early retirement in 1977 after a severe heart attack. Until then I gave many talks on my experiences all over the country, and now – in order to raise money for a Polish Charity in Pruszkow – I will give selected talks. Although I receive many letters from all over the world, it is a source of deep regret that I have never had any real news of my companions. The war did not end as they had anticipated, and they could have been scattered all over the globe. Mr Smith, the American, who was such an inspiration and gentleman, was considerably older than the companions. He may have been working for the American State, and as such would not identify himself. In fact Smith may not have been his real name – remembering that no one spoke English at all. The book was written as a memorial to all those who lived and died for freedom, and who could not speak for themselves. I still sign copies of the book *Remember Always the Precious Heritage of Freedom*.
Slavomir Rawicz, Sandiacre, Notts.

QUESTION: In the Beatles' television film of *All You Need is Love*, someone is holding a placard saying: 'Come back Millie.' Who is/was Millie? Did she come back?

☐ ACCORDING to Mike McCartney in his book *Thank You Very Much* the 'Come back Millie' sign was written in lipstick by one of his relatives, Anne Danher. Millie was Mike and Paul's father's sister, who had gone to Australia – I don't know if she came back!
Alison Fiddler, Fulwood, Preston, Lancs.

☐ I AM the Ann Danher mentioned in Alison Fiddler's answer. I was Millie's great-niece. I am happy to tell you

that Millie, who was visiting her sons in Australia, did come back. She lived on the Wirral for many years where, sadly, she died in 1990. The video went up in a space capsule, so Millie and I are orbiting together. There were others on the video of course – some little pop group – I wonder what happened to them?
Ann Riley (née Danher), Bebington, Wirral.

QUESTION: Whatever happened to the 'Bermuda Triangle'?

☐ IT DISAPPEARED without trace in mysterious circumstances.
Peter Sommer, London N4.

☐ THE Bermuda Triangle, a vaguely defined area in the North Atlantic supposedly associated with a number of unexplained crashes, disappearances and other 'paranormal' phenomena, reached the height of its popularity between 1965–75. Its demise followed the realisation that the number of reported sinkings and other accidents was not at all exceptional for the amount of sea and air traffic that normally passes through the area. Careful analysis of individual incidents showed that logical and familiar explanations could be found for almost all of them, and that there was no more reason to search for a single cause than there would be for all the road accidents in southern England. In what is probably the definitive book on the subject, *The Bermuda Triangle – Mystery Solved* by Lawrence David Kushe, the author concludes: 'The legend of the Bermuda Triangle is a manufactured mystery. It began because of careless research and was elaborated upon and perpetuated by writers who either purposely or unknowingly made use of misconceptions, faulty reasoning and sensationalism. It was repeated so

many times that it began to take on the aura of truth.'
The Bermuda Triangle may no longer be with us but,
for those who need such things, psychic surgery, alien
abductions, spoon bending and corn circles seem to have
proved more than adequate substitutes.
Michael Hutton, Camberwell, London SE5.

□ AS EVERYONE who lives and works in west London will
know, this has shifted to west London. It is now known as
the 'Southall Triangle' and is located near Hayes Bridge.
In spite of a clearly illuminated display, indicating the time
of arrival of the next bus, 207 buses frequently disappear a
minute or so before they are due. Many will also be aware
that all planes approaching or departing from Heathrow
carefully avoid this area.
Eric Parsons, Southall, Middlx.

**QUESTION: Why has the British Army, while patrol-
ling the city streets of Northern Ireland, continued to
wear camouflage designed for the rural environment?
Why has it never been superseded by a more appropriate grey, urban-style uniform?**

□ IT'S nothing to do with camouflage. In the Sudan, they
wore red tunics in the desert and so many were killed. In
world war one they wore khaki, ideal for the Sudan, in green
fields and many were killed. In Belfast they wear rural camouflage, ideal for world war one, but not in the city. It all stems
from British imperial days, when to be seen was enough.
Thomas N. P. Crow, Hillingdon, Middlx.

**QUESTION: Is it true that when milk is heated in
a microwave, the amino acids are turned into toxic**

mirror images of themselves? How dangerous is this to health?

☐ A REPORT in the *Lancet* in 1989 made this claim. The consternation that this must have caused in the boardrooms of the companies that sell milk-based baby foods must have been thunderous! This seemed to be another 'salmonella-in-eggs' problem that curiously did not receive publicity here (though there were newspaper articles in mainland Europe). However, this report was soon followed by numerous other scientific papers stating that the claim was wrong. Nobody could repeat it. It seems to have used the unreasonably alarming information – that the natural (nutritious) L-amino acids in food can be turned into mirror-image versions (D-amino acids) – so as to get the report into the scientific literature. Many fermented-milk products (yoghurt, etc.) and natural foods (shellfish in particular) contain significant amounts of D-amino acids, and evolution has provided us with ways of dealing with them as part of our normal digestive processes.

Dr Graham Barrett, Editor-in-Chief, Amino Acids, *Oxford Brookes University.*

QUESTION: I suffer from large dark spots, lines and splodges floating across my eyes, which impair my otherwise good, glass-corrected sight. Can you tell me what causes this condition and if there is any cure for it?

☐ ACCORDING to *Traditional Chinese Medicine*, 'floaters' are caused by 'blood deficiency', which means that one's blood lacks vitality or 'Qi'. Other signs and symptoms commonly seen alongside floaters are a dull pale face, pale lips, difficulty in getting off to sleep, dizziness and

poor memory. Blood deficiency is more common amongst women than men owing to the strain placed upon the blood by the menses. One of the traditional remedies for blood deficiency in China was to eat more meat and fish, and it is true that one commonly sees blood deficiency in vegetarians and vegans in this country. Acupuncture and herbs are the main remedies, used for at least 2,000 years to treat blood deficiency. You should be careful, however, to ensure that you consult a properly trained practitioner.
Peter Mole, College of Integrated Chinese Medicine, Reading, Berks.

☐ I TOO suffer, except that my splodges are more like fairy lights. Perhaps, like me, the questioner has, in the past, digested several large quantities of a certain kind of mushroom and can still see the after-effects.
Sadie Atkins, Bradford, W. Yorks.

☐ PETER MOLE rightly advises a consultation with a trained practitioner. The symptoms described are probably caused by a posterior vitreous detachment. At birth the vitreous is a homogeneous gel filling the space between the lens and the retina. With time the vitreous partially liquefies. The remaining gel portion separates from the retina and moves around in the liquid. Thickenings in the gel occur wherever the vitreous was strongly attached to the retina, in particular around the optic disc or blind spot. Before the gel liquefies, the thickenings are not noticeable. Once the vitreous becomes mobile the thickenings or floaters come into the line of sight. An uncommon risk is that the mobile gel may only partially separate from the retina and pull on it, so causing a retinal tear or detachment. Traction on the retina causes the patient to experience flashes of light, often noticeable in low-light conditions. Anyone with recent onset of symptoms of floaters or flashes should be seen by an ophthalmologist

to exclude a potentially sight-threatening problem.
Dr Mark Wilkins, ophthalmologist, London SW7.

☐ PETER MOLE may be correct in offering 'blood deficiency' as an acupuncture explanation for floaters in the
eye. His corollary concerning vegetarianism, however,
does not match my experience in acupuncture practice.
Surveying recent years, the majority of patients with
floaters have been meat-eaters. An interesting side issue
is that most of those with floaters have either been smokers
or have lived with smokers.
*Joseph Goodman, Chairman, Council for Acupuncture,
London NW4.*

QUESTION: What is the point of round teabags?

☐ ROUND mugs.
Beth Sibbald, Whitley Bay, Tyne and Wear.

☐ ONLY square teabags have points.
David King, East Dulwich, London.

☐ IF I make my tea with a round teabag, I know I shall
not suffer the taste of Earl Grey tea which, for some
unfathomable reason, my wife favours.
Bill Cawdron, Radyr, Cardiff.

☐ I DON'T know that anyone has yet really got a steer on
this dilemma. As I understand it the round teabag was
an innovation of food technologists at Lyons Tetley in
Woodford around the end of the 1980s. The round teabag
sought finally to do away with two gross shortcomings in
the existing square teabag. Namely: the round bag had
none of the awkward sodden corners which invariably
result, on retrieval from the tea cup, in a depressing

spoor of brown liquid trailing all the way to the pedal
bin. Two: the corners of the traditional square teabag
sometimes harbour recalcitrant tea leaves which resist
infusion and so produce a less than flavourful cuppa.
The round teabag, then, delivers a clean, well-rounded
cup of tea. This is the theory.
Simon Rodway, Olympia, West London.

**QUESTION: In view of the plethora of logos following
privatisation and the 'universitisation' of colleges and
polytechnics, can anyone inform us as to what was
the first recognisable logo, and also when logos first
achieved popularity?**

☐ LOGOS are as old as civilised man and were used by
ancient Egyptians. Trade signs have also been found in the
ruins of Pompeii. Many logos have become official trade
marks, and following the Trade Marks Registration Act of
1875 the coveted number one place was taken by Bass with
its world-famous Red Triangle. But the most recognisable
logo must be the symbol for Christ, denoted simply by
the 22nd letter of the Greek alphabet, X (or chi) – hence,
Xmas. This logo also has a connection with brewing, for
when beer was brewed by monks in the abbeys, they would
swear on the name of Christ as to its excellence, carving
the symbol X on the barrel signifying its quality. Four
Xs meant that it was a real good brew, but some people
wouldn't give a damn about that.
Norman Froggatt, Cheshire.

**QUESTION: Are the footprints and flag left by the first
astronauts to land on the moon still there?**

☐ THE footprints left by Aldrin and Armstrong should

certainly still be there only 25 years after they were made – there is no water or wind on the moon to cause erosion. But, because there is no atmosphere, the surface is completely unprotected against impacts by meteorites of all sizes. This continuous bombardment, especially by microscopic to pinhead-sized particles, gradually pulverises and turns over the uppermost layers of soil. The relatively shallow footprints will look fuzzy in just a few thousand years; in about 1 million years they will be hard to distinguish as footprints; in about 10 million years nearly all traces of them will have vanished. It is harder to predict the resistance of flag material to micrometeorite impacts, although it seems likely to survive its harsh environment in a recognisable state for at least several thousand years.
Dr Mike Dworetsky, Department of Physics and Astronomy, University College, London.

□ I DON'T think the flag left by the first astronauts on the moon will last 'several thousands of years' as predicted by Dr Dworetsky – at least not in its pristine form. The nature of the flag, which was a stock item costing $5.50 purchased through a government supply catalogue meant that it would probably suffer severely from intense sunlight. American flags are made of dye-printed nylon and are notoriously bad at keeping their colours, even in the filtered rays of the sun on the earth's surface. Even if the stall and the crossbar remain, the fabric would fade to complete colourlessness. The flag may not even remain upright, since the post was only sunk about 6–9 inches into the soil, and the film of the lunar module blast-off when the astronauts left suggests that the pole was blown over.
William G. Crampton, Flag Institute, Chester.

QUESTION: Are there many short-sighted animals and why doesn't anybody make them glasses?

□ ACCORDING to my edition of *The Ultimate Irrelevant Encyclopaedia* by Bill Hartston and Jill Dawson: 'The first dog in Spain to be fitted with contact lenses was knocked down and killed by a car the following day. The accident happened in Bilbao. The dog's name was Stan.'
Helen Rigby, London WC1.

□ GOD preserve us from canine opticians. I rely on at least half the vast UK doggie population being short-sighted to enable me to walk down the High Street without having large chunks removed from my ankles every step of the way.
Catherine M. Waterson, Bishopbriggs, Glasgow.

QUESTION: Why, when evolution has ensured that other bodily functions are smooth and painless, is giving birth in humans so excruciatingly painful, troublesome and even life-threatening?

□ HUMANS are the only primates in which the area of a newborn's head is larger than the entrance to the birth canal. Uniquely, the human baby has to corkscrew its way in to the world upside down, facing backwards. Scientists believe this is an unfortunate byproduct of human evolution. Apes emerge facing their mothers, whereas the baby of the intermediate species *Australopithecus* was probably delivered sideways. Apparently, an 'obstetrical dilemma' has occurred in our past. To achieve the upright stance of the hunter-gatherer, the pelvis needed to become narrower. However, the human brain evolved at such a rate that our brain-to-body size ratio doubled, causing the tight squeeze we experience today.
Jeff Craig, Edinburgh.

□ THE BOOK OF GENESIS states that God created man as

'male and female, in his own image' and then told them they were free to eat from any tree except the 'tree of the knowledge of good and evil'. When they disobeyed, God's question to the woman, 'What is this you have done?' is followed by the statement, 'because you have done this . . . I will greatly increase your pains in childbearing; with pain you will give birth to children.'
Philip Miles, Hove, E. Sussex.

□ As a mother of three, I tend to favour the slightly more cynical view that giving birth needs to be as painful, troublesome and life-threatening as possible in order to toughen up the mother for 18-plus years of 'more of the same'.
Helen Day, Guisborough, Cleveland.

QUESTION: What is the origin of the expression 'sold down the river'?

□ In 19th-century US, slavery was concentrated in the cotton- and tobacco-growing areas of the Deep South. The expression 'sold down the river' originated in the slave states, and referred to the treatment of slaves who tried to escape to the free northern states. This involved sending them further down the Mississippi river for sale, deeper into the south where the chances of absconding were remote.
Jane Richardson, Groeslon, Caernarfon, Gwynedd.

□ Mark Twain's novel *Pudd'nhead Wilson* highlights the fear which many slaves had of the river. Judge Driscoll is trying to identify who stole his money. He says to his slaves: 'I give you one minute. If at the end of that time you have not confessed, I will sell you down the river!' The author then writes: 'It was equivalent to sending them to

hell! No Missouri negro doubted this. Roxy reeled in her tracks and the colour vanished out of her face; the others dropped to their knees as if they had been shot . . .'
Harry Morgan, Edinburgh.

QUESTION: When someone phones me on my mobile phone, how does the network know where I am? Does it broadcast across the whole country?

☐ THE system is constantly tracking the location of all 'switched on' mobile phones and updating their location on a whereabouts database. Additionally the whereabouts table is advised where you are when you switch your phone on, and as you pass from one cellular radio station area to another. When a call is made to your cellular number, the system refers to the whereabouts table appropriate to your number and picks out the area in which you were last registered. The system then activates the radio stations (called cells) to send out a signal to alert your phone. When the phone responds, a ring signal is sent to make the phone ring and a radio channel line is established for the call. In the early days of cellular radio, there was often a long wait before the caller received the ringing tone because, if you had switched off your telephone, the system tried adjacent areas to see if you had moved there. The system now checks your location more regularly and if you cannot be found (i.e. the phone is switched off or out of the coverage area) it is assumed that you are not available. Some systems then recommend that the caller tries again, because the mobile phone may have just moved to a new area and not yet registered its new whereabouts.
Sarah M. Todd, Surbiton, Surrey.

QUESTION: Somewhere in a field in the north of

England there used to be a sign saying: 'Please do not throw stones at this notice.' Are there any other examples of this kind of helpful public information?

☐ AT A seminary in Ibadan, Nigeria, a sign posted over a telephone on a landing of the staircase in the staff residence read: 'This telephone is to not be used for either incoming or outgoing calls.' (Subsequently, the phone was stolen, but the sign remained.)
Calvin H. Poulin, Nairobi.

☐ THIS notice was posted at the Dunbar (Vancouver) Post Office: 'For your added convenience, this Post Office will be closed on Saturdays.'
Hulbert Silver, Vancouver.

☐ WRITTEN around the edge of my son's 'I am 2' badge taken from a birthday card are the words: 'Unsuitable for children under 3 years of age.'
Jane Fallows, Gordonvale, Queensland.

☐ OUTSIDE Stafford prison there is a sign which reads: 'Long Stay Car Park'.
Frank Nowikowski, Buenos Aires.

☐ ROADSIGN in the former Transkei homeland: 'When this sign is under water, this bridge is impassable.'
Laura Yeatman, Johannesburg.

☐ WHILE crossing Quito, Ecuador, by bus, I noted the following message written in Spanish on a wall at the side of a busy thoroughfare: 'Warning to Motorists: Reading graffiti is a frequent cause of traffic accidents.'
Raymond Denson, Ontario.

☐ IN A village hall in Kent there is a notice: 'In the event

of fire, evacuate the hall and call the Fire Service.' The nearest public telephone box to this hall is opposite the fire station.
Tony McColgan, Hull, N. Humberside.

☐ SOME time ago I received some junk mail which was addressed to 'The Occupier, 33 Easton House', etc. Above the address was the instruction: 'If addressee has moved, please return to sender, giving new address.'
Richard Phillips, Bath, Avon.

☐ THERE is a sign in a lion park in Australia (normally viewed from the safety of a motor car) which reads:

> Adults: $5
> Children: $2
> Poms on bicycles: Free

J. G. Shelley, Vaucluse, Australia.

☐ SEEN on a motorway in Vermont, US: 'Rest area ahead. No rest rooms.'
Guy Johnston, Kirchhundem, Germany.

☐ SIGN on a farm gate near Oyen, Alberta: 'We shoot every third salesman.'
J. C. Haigh, Saskatchewan, Canada.

☐ NOTED at a service station along the main highway between Sydney and Melbourne: 'Due to unavoidable delays, this service station will not be closing until the 1st of August.'
Rob Wetselaar, Canberra.

☐ STANDING in the water, 20 feet away from the beach in a state park in southern Florida, is a row of signs each

carrying the same message: 'No Wading or Swimming. Do Not Feed the Alligators.'
David G. Onn, Newark, Delaware.

QUESTION: Is anyone, or, apart from Adolf and his family, has anyone, ever been called 'Hitler'?

☐ UP UNTIL 18 months ago, the Hitler and Son Ltd jewellery shop in Paphos, Cyprus, seemed to be doing quite well – although I can't say I bought any of the jewellery!
Fran Manhire, Wales.

☐ AS CHAPLAIN to the English-speaking congregation in the Sultanate of Oman for three years, I had the privilege on many occasions to celebrate Communion at a small early Sunday morning service for someone called Hitler. Often in the same congregation was Winston. They were both from the Indian sub-continent, born in the early 1940s; their parents presumably came out on opposite sides as to whom they supported. For some Indian nationalists, Hitler was clearly a hero.
Revd Ray Skinner, St Lawrence Church, Surrey.

☐ FIVE years ago, a mechanic called Hitler repaired my vehicle in a garage near Lake Constance in southern Germany – and did a good job quickly. I have told this story to colleagues who expressed great surprise that anyone should have kept that name. They explained that, in Germany, the process to change your name is complicated, bureaucratic and slow but that a person called Hitler could get it changed very quickly and most had done so.
E. W. Grunby, Sheffield.

☐ HITLER was not born this but, as everyone knows, Schicklgrüber. However, some years ago I looked up the 'H' in the Vienna telephone directory and found a couple of Hilters. A tactical change of name perhaps?
Daniel S. Allen, Bristol.

☐ IN MY many years as a missionary, I have quite frequently had to baptise Hitlers and Lenins. The Peruvian custom of pulling foreign names out of calendars, almanacs and newspapers, pronouncing them as written and with no awareness of their associations, makes me grimace every time we hold a baptismal ceremony. There used to be an old rule that every child had to have a 'Christian' name but, unlike some of my colleagues, I have never insisted on it: parents have their rights and there might someday be a Saint Hitler.
Revd Gerard Hanlon, Iquitos, Peru.

QUESTION: In Sue Townsend's book *The Queen and I*, the Republican Party gained power by broadcasting subliminal messages to persuade the public to vote for them. What would be the likely result of such a strategy in reality?

☐ SIXTEEN years of uninterrupted Tory government.
Bill Cronshaw, Gloucester.

QUESTIONS: Can any creatures other than man be said to commit rape?

☐ IT IS somewhat difficult to ask them, isn't it?
Charlie Holmes, Newcastle upon Tyne.

☐ CHARLIE HOLMES is too flippant. Maybe the question was prompted by a need to find if man has an inherent propensity for evil which, like our supposed superior intelligence, sets us apart from other animals. This is a philosophical question far beyond the original query, but there is no need to 'ask' animals if they have experienced rape. Many years ago, on the towpath at Barnes, south-west London, I noticed two mallards mating in the shallows. The drake was pecking the duck's head, presumably to keep her submissive. As soon as the drake had finished, he was replaced by another who also pecked the duck, forcing her head into the water with what seemed to be practised violence. There were five or six other drakes quacking nearby, probably waiting their turn. Later, when walking back, I found the duck drowned in about 1 inch of water. While this might have been a 'natural' event, it was as near to a gang-rape as one can imagine and it certainly contained all the elements of violence, subjugation, peer encouragement and so on that are identifiable in some of the worst excesses of man.

Ray Hennessy, Woodley, Berks.

☐ RAPE or 'forced copulation' has been documented in a number of diverse animal species from mallard ducks to scorpion flies and from crab-eater seals to white-fronted bee-eaters. The fact that males of other species also commit rape has led the American sociobiologists Randy and Nancy Thornhill to suggest that it may be an evolved 'reproductive strategy' used by some males who would otherwise be unable to gain a mate and pass their genes on. Another possibility is that rape occurs in some males (animal and human) as a maladaptive consequence of males, in general, being sexually aroused more rapidly than females.

Dr Lance Workman, lecturer in Biological Psychology, University of Glamorgan.

QUESTION: How can I straighten the bent aerial on my car without it snapping?

☐ TAKE hold of the said aerial below the bend with the thumb and first two fingers of the right hand. With the same two fingers of the left hand, take hold of the aerial above the bend. Think very hard about Uri Geller.
D. M. O'Rourke, Lancs.

QUESTION: At what stage in cinema history were the simple words 'The End' replaced by four miles of credits that about four people stay behind to read? And why?

☐ I CAN remember when 'The Queen' was played at the end of every cinema showing, prompting a disorderly rush to get out before the end of the credits, and the habit has stayed. Credits are primarily an ego trip but also help when negotiating fees and have an effect on residual payments. Television has solved the problem of self-multiplying credits by spooling them past too fast to read, but the cinema has more time to spare and they help to get the punters out. The four people who stay behind may be looking for the names of friends or colleagues, but are more likely proclaiming their supposed Show Business membership to the other three.
David Brinicombe, retired film sound recordist, Ealing, London.

☐ THIS dates from the demise in the 1960s of the dream-factory studio system. In that era, the functions and services which are now so laboriously listed were simply part of the fixed infrastructure of the studio operation, and the persons performing them were salaried employees working in a relatively secure and stable environment. In those circumstances they had no incentive to

claim on-screen credits. Now, the studios have essentially become rental facilities, with the infrastructure fragmented into competing contracted-out service providers; thus even caterers are only as good as their last round of sandwiches and need credits to survive in their competitive world.
Bernard Hrusa-Marlow, Morden, Surrey.

☐ CLOSING credits on films are treated with proper respect in Paris, where cinema is an art form. However long they may last, they are sat through reverently by Parisians who vocally deprecate the indecent haste with which Anglo-Saxon visitors make for the exits.
Henry Cleere, Paris.

QUESTION: Many houses in Bath built from the 1770s onward have beautiful stone staircases in which it is not easy to see how the outer ends are supported. Apparently, such designs are banned under current building regulations on the grounds that their 'structural logic' cannot be proved. If this is true, is it because the regulations are fatuous, or because the likes of Brunel never bothered to work it out and today's structural engineers aren't much cop?

☐ CANTILEVERED stone stairs are not banned under the current building regulations. Stairs we build for sheltered housing are built from individual artificial stone (precast concrete) treads which are simply built into the walls, each tread resting on the one below it. The structural logic of these stairs is difficult to prove because the weight of the treads and people using the stairs is not carried by one element, but is shared by the walls and the lower treads of the stair. The walls also prevent the treads from twisting out of position. The engineers of these stairs were

able to persuade the building control officers that these
stairs could stand up by explaining where the loads were
distributed and by using historical examples of similar
stairs which have successfully stood for centuries, such as
Inigo Jones's Tulip Stair at the Queens House, Greenwich,
which was built in the 1620s.
*Peter Ranken, architect, Hunt Thompson Associates,
London.*

□ WE HAVE built quite a number of new staircases using
the principles and details of the old ones. The treads were
made either of very good-quality precast concrete or of
stone. Two of these staircases were load-tested in order
to allay the fears of an unconvinced Building Inspector.
They supported several tons of bagged cement with barely
perceptible deflection.
*Sam Price, consultant engineer, Price and Myers Con-
sulting Engineers, London.*

□ I WOULD suggest that the questioner looks around him
and marvels at such structures as Waterloo International
Station, the 'air rights' buildings at Charing Cross and
Liverpool Street stations, the Hongkong and Shanghai
Bank, the new terminus at Stansted Airport, the Renault
building at Swindon, the UK Pavilion at Expo '92 . . . the
list is almost endless. Today's structural engineers have
skill, flair and ingenuity!
*Paul Tanner, consultant engineer, Scott-White and
Hookins, Hants.*

**QUESTIONS: Are humans the only creatures capable
of picking their noses? Do other species suffer any
inconvenience as a result of their handicap?**

□ I WOULD like to point out that cows can *lick* their

nostrils. I doubt that cows envy us our nose-cleaning abilities, and I certainly do not envy them theirs.
Jeremy C. Henty, Cambridge.

☐ ON THIS question, I inherited a mangy, disreputable 38-year-old cockatoo who not only picks his nose, but then uses the same claw to clean the debris from inside his beak. I've tried leaving a hankie and toothbrush handy, but the old reprobate flings them to the floor the first chance he gets.
Trish Colton, Leeds.

☐ LAST Saturday at London Zoo, I saw a gorilla picking her nose and eating it, much to the horror of the assembled human audience.
A. F. Wilson, London Zoo Lifewatch member, London N4.

☐ COCKATOOS are great mimics. Trish Colton, whose cockatoo picks its nose and then pushes its claw into its beak, should ask herself where it got the idea from!
Ray Hennessy, Woodley, Berks.

QUESTION: VCRs can be programmed to record up to eight hours of television. Why is there no equivalent device for the radio? Will the advent of digital radio make it possible, theoretically, to download radio programmes into a computer?

☐ IF, HAVING been suitably tuned, a radio-cassette recorder is put into its record mode and connected to the mains supply via a time switch, then recording will be delayed until the moment when the time switch turns the power on. Regrettably this straightforward procedure cannot be recommended, as leaving a recorder set to record without the mechanism running is liable to cause damage by deforming the rubber pressure roller. Also, the small audio-cassettes cannot provide anything like the recording times available from a video-cassette, although their recording quality is generally higher. There is absolutely no reason why VCRs cannot have radio tuners built into them to record radio programmes under timer control in the same way as is possible with TV programmes, but machines of this type do not seem to be available. However, if you have a VCR whose timer can be programmed to record from audio and video inputs, the output from a radio or radio tuner can be fed into the VCR's audio input for recording, and the timer set in the usual way. However, the mechanics of the video-recording process demand that a video signal be fed into the VCR in addition to an audio signal. One way of satisfying this requirement is to use the 'video output' signal generated by a computer for display on a video monitor. Alternatively, persuade a friend to record your radio programme for you manually in the traditional way! The answer to the questioner's second point is that it is already feasible, using comparatively inexpensive equipment, to download radio programmes to a computer's hard disk. You can use an Apple Macintosh program called HyperCard II. This has the capacity to record and store in digital form, sounds lasting a minute or more (maximum duration being determined by the amount of RAM available). While this is too short to record a complete radio programme, the programme could be transferred to the computer in sections from a tape recording, and then a HyperCard 'script' can be written to replay these in their correct sequence automatically.

Professor Brian Josephson, Department of Physics, University of Cambridge.

☐ THE questioner is wrong in his assumption that there is no device to record eight hours of radio. My Bang &

Olufsen System 5500 allows 'multiple-event' recording of programmes, from one or more radio stations. The system is linked to a B & O video-cassette recorder, which records audio (including radio) at half-speed. Hence an E240 video cassette will hold eight hours of radio, and the VCR can be pre-programmed, just as it is for recording television.
P. Clift, Bolton.

□ THE only decent radio programmes worth recording are the speech programmes on BBC Radio 4. Since this station has only 12 per cent reach in the UK, and no quality speech station exists in America or Japan, why should the main manufacturers design and sell a radio-auto-recorder on video lines, even with the existing technology?
Peter Baker, researcher, Granada TV.

□ PROFESSOR BRIAN JOSEPHSON is wrong on one point and misleading on two others. Firstly, a video signal is not required to record audio (certainly not on any video I've encountered). Secondly, while a standard video produces very poor audio, the quality of reproduction on a hi-fi video is way in excess of most audio equipment! For best results the user should seek a video with a manual record level. Thirdly, most modern hi-fi cassette decks have a Timer Play/Record switch coupled with servo controls. These, used with a mains time switch, can record or play without the problem of compressing the pressure (or pinch) roller.
Steve Epps, Great Yarmouth, Norfolk.

□ PROFESSOR JOSEPHSON'S reply is incomplete and, in some respects, misleading. While it may be true that the only way to record radio programmes on a simple radio-cassette player involves potentially damaging the rubber pinch wheel, more advanced hi-fi recorders have

provision to be set in a standby 'timed record' mode, with the pinch roller free, which starts the recording when the power is switched on by an external timer. There are many inexpensive suitable timers on the market which allow recordings to be made from a radio tuner coupled to the recorder at a number of times over a period of a week. Using a C120 tape with an auto-reverse recorder, a recording lasting up to two hours can be made. For longer recordings, as Professor Josephson says, a VCR can be used, with a radio tuner coupled to the audio input and using the VCR's own timer. However, there is absolutely no need to provide a video signal when using the VCR in this mode – I have recorded the whole of *Die Meistersinger* in this way without problems.
Harold Stern, Ealing, London W13.

QUESTION: What makes the earth rotate?

□ LOVE makes the World go round. Sex makes the Earth move.
Arthur Wren, Surrey.

□ THE short answer is 'statistics' plus 'conservation'. The 'clumpiness' of matter at every scale in the visible universe – planets (including earth), stars (including sun), galaxies (including Milky Way) – has resulted from the action of gravity, causing small *statistical* irregularities to grow, as slightly denser-than-average regions suck in surrounding matter. Now we've all seen skaters start a spin, slow it by spreading out their arms, and then speed up again by bringing their arms down to their sides: that's *conservation of angular momentum* at work; and exactly the same happens as these astronomical clumps of matter form. Each bit of captured matter adds to (or subtracts from)

the angular momentum of the growing planet, etc.; and *statistics* make it extremely unlikely that all these bits of angular momentum will exactly balance – so planets, stars, galaxies all rotate. In the case of highly condensed bodies such as planets, frictional forces resulting from events such as tides can gradually dissipate the rotation (just as the skater will eventually come to rest because of friction between skate and ice).
J. D. Lewin, Oxford.

QUESTION: Is it possible to get tanned through glass?

☐ No. TO get a tan requires exposure to ultraviolet radiation, whether from the sun or any other source. Glass is effective in screening out ultraviolet radiation.
Peter Hughes, London E17.

☐ YES, most definitely. Many people with curtains will notice that they tend to fade where sunlight has fallen through a glazed window directly on to the fabric. The fabric not directly exposed to the sunlight fades at a much slower rate. The bleaching of curtains is a result of mainly ultraviolet B (UVB) light that the glass cannot block. UVB is the main cause of sunburn, although UVA used in sunbeds will tan but not burn. 'Laminated glass' as used in car windscreens and 'risk areas' in buildings is made of a sandwich of glass and Polyvinylbutaryl (PVB). Manufacturers of PVB claim that this can block up to 99 per cent of UVB. Use of laminated glass in windows will certainly reduce fading in curtains and help reduce sunburn of those who wish to sunbathe in the comfort of their own living room.
Noah Shepherd, Phuket, Thailand.

220   *Notes & Queries*

□ PETER HUGHES says it is not possible. So, if they don't use glass to make the fluorescent tubes for sun beds, what do they use?
Ian Joyce, Furzton, Bucks.

□ HOW come, Mr Hughes, that my arm was tanned on a coach journey from Liverpool to Manchester? I've even got the white bits to prove it!
John Cole, Liverpool.

QUESTION: Is there or was there ever a distinction between Bosnia and Hercegovina, be it territorial, ethnic or other?

□ BOSNIA and Hercegovina were originally distinct south Slav territories. Bosnia was largely Catholic and allied to Croatia. Hercegovina was largely Orthodox and allied to Serbia. The populations of both became increasingly mixed after the Turkish conquest, and Orthodox Serbs eventually became the largest ethnic group in both Bosnia and Hercegovina. Bosnia and Hercegovina were transferred together from the Turkish empire to the Austrian in 1878 and the two of them later constituted one of the republics of post-war Yugoslavia. Maps rarely show where Bosnia ends and Hercegovina begins, but one exception can be found in Noel Malcolm's *Bosnia: A Short History*.
Dave Buckner, Bearsden, Glasgow.

QUESTION: A friend recently told me that the term for a group of ravens is 'an unkindness'. Are there any other similarly bizarre names for groups of animals?

□ MIGHT I suggest a 'filling' of dentists and a 'sewer' of lawyers.
A. J. G. de Billwiller-Kiss, San Francisco.

QUESTION: Joan of Arc – Arc of What? Why?

☐ THE name Arc has its basis in the Greek word *arctos*, meaning the bear – more particularly the constellation of the Great Bear from which the English word arctic is derived. The pertinence of the word bear to Joan of Arc lies in the probability that she was of the Merovingian bloodline, i.e. a direct descendant of the offspring of Jesus and the Magdalene. The head of the Merovingian line in any generation received the title Prince Ursus (the Lord Bear). The legend is that Mary Magdalene left the Holy Land soon after the Crucifixion and, pregnant with the child of Jesus, landed in Provence at Les Saintes Maries de la Mer, thereby bringing with her the Royal Blood (the Sang Réal or Sangraal – mistranslated as Holy Grail – to initiate the story as handed down to us through Wolfram von Eschenbach and Wagner). So it would seem that Joan of Arc, as well as confirming the prophecy of the Maid of Lorraine, had the additional panache of a blood-link with the Son of God himself. Hence the aura of extreme holiness which has always surrounded her name. The Merovingian connection would also explain the mystery of Joan of Arc's execution. She was a menace to all three parties concerned: the Roman Church and its obsession with celibacy, for whom the idea of a Priapic Jesus is a dreadful heresy; the English for whom she was a national threat; and Charles VII of France, who did not try to rescue her once she had performed her 'miracle' of expelling the English, since she was much closer to the true line of succession than the House of Valois.
Roly Atnod, Brighton, E. Sussex.

☐ THE points made about Joan the Maid's surname are interesting but rather pointless as she was not Jacques d'Arc's daughter and never gave d'Arc as her name. Since the discovery at the Vatican of a very interesting document on her origin by Edward Schneider, a number of post-war French historians have made a convincing case making Joan the illegitimate daughter of Isabel of Bavaria, the adulterous Queen of France, and her equally adulterous brother-in-law Louis d'Orleans. If this sounds like an extravagant claim, be warned that it is only the first of a number of revelations about the French heroine in Dr N. Wooster's well-researched book *The Real Joan of Arc?* (1992, The Book Guild) which contends, backed by substantial evidence and a dozen French historians, that Joan was not burnt at the stake!

G. Richeux, Hatfield, Herts.

☐ Is ROLY ATNOD kidding us and should we read his name backwards to get Don Taylor? There is little contemporary documentary evidence for Joan of Arc's life, and most of it comes from the records of her trial for heresy and sorcery. *Chambers Biographical Dictionary* does not mention any link with the Merovingians though it makes note of the sources, and nor do any of the notable histories of the period such as Christopher Allmand's *The Hundred Years War* (CUP, 1988) which, on the contrary, states that she was 'an unknown peasant girl from Lorraine'. *The Oxford Companion to English Literature* says her name is spelt Jeanne Darc (no apostrophe) and that she was the daughter of Jacques Darc, a farmer of Domremy in the valley of the Meuse. The name is more likely to derive from *arc*, the French for bow, indicating that her ancestors were bowmen or bowyers, than from the Greek *arktos*.

G. R. Hulme, Leicester.

☐ MR ATNOD failed to point out that most historians have concluded that d'Arc is derived from Joan's father's birthplace – which seems to have been either Arc-en-Barrois or

Art-sur-Meurthe, the weight of evidence pointing to the former. And there is no absolute certainty that d'Arc is the correct form of the name. In documents relating to Jeanne's life it is variously spelled d'Arc, Darc, Dart, Dar, Daix, Daiz, Day, d'Ay and Tart. This does not appear to detract from the majority consensus mentioned above, the discrepancies being explained by reference to a pronunciation idiosyncrasy in the Lorraine region.

J. Patterson, London SE19.

QUESTION: What is the origin of the 'Jack' in Union Jack, and under what circumstances is the Union Jack flown on board ship?

☐ THE Union Jack consists of the Union Flag bordered all round with a narrow white border. It is flown from the jackstaff in the eyes of the bows of Royal Navy ships, and in this place only. It is never flown ashore. What is flown from public buildings and private houses is properly known as the Union Flag, which is never flown at sea.

L. W. Hammond, Sudbury, Suffolk.

☐ L. W. HAMMOND was a bit over-pedantic. The Union Jack is flown on Royal Navy ships as a mark of nationality. It is also worn on any ship carrying an Admiral of the Fleet or on which a court-martial is taking place, and was at one time part of the range of signals used by the Navy. For these reasons it cannot be used as a national flag by civilian vessels, which have to use the Red Ensign. Civilian vessels can, however, use the Union Jack with a white border as described by Mr Hammond (the one used by the Navy has no white border). There is no law that says the plain flag when used on land has to be called the Union Flag

– that is simply a custom which grew up in the Army. Scouts, Guides and the Government itself have referred to the flag as the Union Jack for a long time, and the name has become established as an affectionate nickname for our national flag, both on land and at sea. As to the origins of the term, the answer is that nobody knows. Some attribute it very speculatively to King 'Jacques' in whose reign it was introduced, although why his name has to be rendered in French is left unexplained. Others think that 'jack' is a term for a small version of an object. From about 1630 the flag began to be flown from the bowsprit rather than from the mainmast of a naval vessel, and it is possible that it received its name at that time. The first recorded instance of the term is in 1633. The following year Sir Nathaniel Boteler, referring to the flag, wrote: 'Every such vessel . . . is permitted and enjoined to wear one of these in a small volume in her bowsprit's top.' That has been the case ever since.

William G. Crampton, Director, Flag Institute, Chester.

□ I AM afraid L. W. Hammond was incorrect. The Union Flag with a white border is the Pilot Jack which may be worn by any British-registered ship in harbour and wearing her ensign. It is, in fact, very rarely seen.

Robert Moore, Holywell, Clwyd.

QUESTION: Is there any reason why the United States, as a former British colony, couldn't, or shouldn't, be a member of the Commonwealth?

□ THE Commonwealth came into existence in 1926 as a formal alliance of Britain, Australia, New Zealand, South Africa, Canada and the Irish Free State. All were described as 'autonomous communities within the British Empire

. . . united by a common allegiance to the Crown'. As former British colonies became independent, they too asked to join, although in many cases without showing any particular allegiance to the Crown. The United States of America (not a former British colony but 13 of them), having won its independence in 1776, could not have been in the original 1926 Commonwealth nor would it have seen any reason to ask to join later on, having no recent connection to Britain and having been getting along on its own pretty well since the 18th century.
Walter Millis, London W9.

□ THIS possibility was foreseen by Bernard Shaw in *The Apple Cart* (1929) in which the United States tears up the Declaration of Independence and applies to become part of the British Empire. The King rejects the invitation to become Emperor of America on the grounds that Britain will be swallowed up, becoming a kind of reservation for sentimental Americans. Shaw is right on both counts. The United States could certainly apply to join the Commonwealth if it repealed the Declaration of Independence, but if it didn't we would survive, as the King says, 'only as another star on your flag'.
Laurie Smith, Carshalton, Surrey.

QUESTION: My son recently took a swimming personal survival test where he had to take his clothes off in the water, tie knots in them, inflate them and use them as floats. Is there any record of anyone using this technique to survive in water?

□ ACCORDING to Richard O'Kane in *Clear the Bridge* (Rand McNally, 1977), Lieutenant Larry Savadkin escaped from the flooded conning tower of the United States submarine Tang on 25 October 1944. Sailing in the Formosa

Strait, she had been hit by her own malfunctioning torpedo. Savadkin tied a knot in the bottom of each trouser leg, then, swinging the trousers above the sea, trapped air in them and used them as water wings, repeating the procedure as necessary when the air slowly leaked out. He was rescued by the Japanese after eight hours in the water.
David Silverson, Henfield, W. Sussex.

☐ AT 12 years old I attempted the Gold Award of this test. After completing many lengths and then having to swim through two hoops at the bottom of the deep end, fully dressed, I can safely say that sticking my chin into the crutch of a pair of inflated trousers was the only way I could prevent myself from sinking with exhaustion. I'm sure whenever I happen to be ship-wrecked in the middle of the ocean, the techniques I practised will come flooding back.
Jane Weaver, South Woodford, London E18.

QUESTION: How can you tell when invisible ink has run out?

☐ THE solution is clear.
Mrs D. Warren, Stevenage, Herts.

☐ WHEN the CIA stops sending you cheques.
Jason Balantine-Scott, Notting Hill, London.

QUESTION: Why can't I wash my hair with soap, i.e. why do I need shampoo?

☐ IF YOU want to remove dirt from your hair, either soap or shampoo – even washing-up liquid or soap powder –

will do the job. They are all surfactants, chemicals that can dislodge dirt and grease. The difference between these substances lies in their power at removing dirt — soap is more powerful than shampoo, and more than is really needed for cleaning hair. Hair is naturally slightly acidic, so shampoos are often made slightly acidic as well (what is meant by pH-balanced). Soap is alkaline, but if you did wash your hair with it, you could restore the smoothness by rinsing it with a weak acid, using a conditioner or even just lemon juice. However, it is questionable as to whether even shampoo is necessary. The scalp secretes sebum to lubricate and protect the hair, and this on its own washes away dirt. Shampoo removes the sebum, so the skin responds by producing more. This is why the more you wash hair the greasier it may become. If you stop washing hair completely there may be a short-lived phase of greasiness, but a natural balance soon appears and the hair then keeps itself in a perfect, naturally clean state. But the shampoo manufacturers wouldn't like us to know that, would they?

Bryan Hopkins, Sheffield.

QUESTION: There is an area in the Suffolk region known as the 'Tattingstone Wonder'. Can anyone explain how this name came about?

☐ THE Tattingstone Wonder is not an area, but a building. We have owned and lived in this property for the last 13 years. Built in the 18th century, it comprises three workers' cottages with the façade of a church built around three sides. From the rear it looks like a row of cottages with a hollow tower; from the front like a church. An entry from *Follies, a Guide to Rogue Architecture* reads: 'The blessed inhabitants of the village of Tattingstone were silly enough in 1790 for the local squire, Edward White, to vow

to give them something they could really gawp at. Thus
came the Tattingstone Wonder, one of the most famous
follies in Britain. It started life as a pair of cottages,
until Squire White decided to enliven the view from
Tattingstone Place. He built a third cottage on the end
and topped it with a square flint church tower, omitting
the southern wall because it wasn't visible from the house.
The front of the cottages was replaced by a façade with two
Gothick windows, and the crowning touch was a large rose
window on the south-eastern wall.'
Helen and Stephen Solley, London E9.

**QUESTION: Suppose members of the Government
since 1979, rather than being committed politicians,
had in fact been foreign agents or malevolent aliens
intent on destroying the social fabric and industrial
base of Britain. In what ways would they have acted
differently?**

☐ THEY wouldn't have dared do what the Thatcher
and Major Governments have done, for fear of being
found out.
Alan Burkett-Gray, Blackheath, London SE3.

☐ SURELY malevolent aliens capable of interplanetary travel
would be intelligent enough to make themselves resemble
likeable human beings? Foreign agents, I can't help thinking,
would almost certainly possess more style and wit. Unfortunately, I believe that for the last 16 years the destruction of
our country has been carried out by the real Enemy Within.
D. C. Godfrey, Twickenham, Surrey.

☐ THEY would have returned home, some time ago,
mission accomplished.
Jackie Bryant, Winchester, Hants.

QUESTION: What are the lyrics of 'La Bamba' as sung by Ritchie Valens, and what do they mean?

□ THE words in the version I have (by the Colombian band La Sonora Dinamita) are:

> *Para bailar La Bamba se necesita*
> *Una poca de gracia para mi, para ti.*
> *Ay arriba y arriba por ti sere*
> *Por ti sere.*
> *Yo no soy marinero – soy capitan,*
> *La, La Bamba,*

(plus a bit of yodelling and whooping), which I assume to mean:

> To dance La Bamba requires
> A little gracefulness for me and for you.
> [I will be over/above you.]
> I am not (just) a seaman, I'm the captain.
> La, La Bamba, etc.

I don't know what 'La Bamba' itself means, but *'bambolear'* is 'to swing or sway'.
John Phillips, Neath Hill, Bucks.

□ ACCORDING to the sleeve-notes of the Rhino Records compilation album *The Best of La Bamba* (RC 70617), the song has no birth certificate though it undoubtedly originated in Veracruz on the Gulf Coast of Mexico in the 17th century as a blend of Spanish and African styles. DJ John Peel's historic spoken word recording of the lyric mistakenly translates *bamba* as 'goat'. The word is, however, probably derived from the African/Puerto Rican musical style called *bomba*. The Rhino LP also suggests

bamba may be a corruption of *banda*, a sash worn by male dancers in Veracruz. What is certain is that 'La Bamba' is one of the best-known songs in the world, suitable for adaptation to any style, from traditional Veracruz *jarocho* to heavy metal. I've heard it played from Bulawayo to Ulan Bator and collected dozens of versions of the tune, including a recording I made in Mali, West Africa, of a balafon interpretation. The BBC Gramophone Library has a collection of 187 'La Bambas' which include ill-advised recordings by Elvis Costello's dad (Ross McManus with the Joe Loss Orchestra), Eartha Kitt, Dusty Springfield, Shirley Bassey and the Mormon Tabernacle Choir.
Andy Kershaw, London W1.

QUESTION: Is there any connection between Turkey (as in the name of the country) and turkey (as in the bird)?

☐ THE turkey originally came from Mexico and the West Indies, where it was known as the *uexolotl* and offered to Columbus and his crew on his fourth voyage in 1502. Columbus himself referred to the delicacy as *gallina de la tierra* and praised its flavour. The birds were transported back to Spain in 1511 for farming, and a pair were sent to Rome in 1520. Levant merchants, calling in at ports in Spain, carried these odd-looking 'chickens of the earth' to Britain. But people confused the West Indies with the East Indies and christened them 'turkie-cocks', assuming that they had been discovered by Vasco da Gama, the Portuguese explorer who was the first European to sail across the Indian Ocean. This misunderstanding persisted throughout most of northern Europe and even into the Middle East, where the birds were eventually introduced. To the French, the turkey was known as the *coq d'Inde*

('cock of India') and to the Scandinavians as *Kalkon*, which was a specific reference to Calicut, the first Indian city that da Gama visited. Even in Turkey, the bird was called the *hindi* and attributed to India. Only in India itself, where the new discovery was known as the *peru*, did the name offer a reasonable approximation of geographical origins.
Rhys H. Hughes, Cardiff.

QUESTION: Tobacco smoking is now accompanied by health warnings and advertising bans. Yet the drinking of alcohol, which can be equally injurious, is not. Why?

☐ WHILST there are no warnings on alcoholic drinks in the UK, I recently noticed the following on an American wine bottle: 'Government warning: (1) According to the Surgeon General women should not drink alcoholic beverages during pregnancy because of the risk of birth defects. (2) Consumption of alcoholic beverages impairs your ability to drive a car or operate machinery, and may cause health problems.' This warning is not on American wines sold in the UK, but it does appear elsewhere outside the US.
Dr Christopher Williams, Bristol.

QUESTION: What was the name of the play being performed at the Ford Theater when Abraham Lincoln was assassinated?

☐ THE play was *Our American Cousin*, a British comedy which had been touring the US since 1858 as a vehicle for its British actress star Laura Keene. Never performed since, it was based on the theme of money-grabbing Brits

latching on to an American backwoodsman whom they
take to be their long-lost wealthy relative. John Wilkes
Booth, Lincoln's assassin, knew the play well. He timed
his attack on the president for a moment when he knew
there would be only one actor on stage: Harry Hawk,
an American comedian and Laura Keene's manager, who
played the backwoodsman Asa Trenchard. The shooting
happened during the second act at the point just after
the Brits have discovered Trenchard actually has no
money at all and storm out, leaving him alone on stage
muttering revenge. The last words Lincoln actually heard
were Trenchard's curse: 'Well I guess I know enough to
turn you inside out, you sockdologizing old mantrap!'
Immediately afterwards the audience heard a shot and
watched Booth leap from the presidential box on to the
stage – breaking his ankle in the process – and hobble
past an astonished Hawk.
Steve Bates, London W3.

**QUESTION: If all people world-wide were to stop
eating meat and become vegetarian, would there be
enough non-meat products available to feed the world's
population?**

☐ IF MORE people became vegetarian, a larger number
could be fed. If everyone in the world were to give up
meat in favour of a grain-based diet – and food evenly
distributed – the world could support 6 billion people
at the UN recommended calorie level. If Americans were
to reduce their meat consumption by 10 per cent, they
would each year free over 12 million tons of grain
for human consumption – enough to feed adequately
all the 60 million people who will starve to death
this year.
Anne Benewick, London W1.

☐ THE food would be fairly dull and basic, but variety

could be achieved by industry producing synthetic and manufactured products. The world would also have to allow food to be grown instead of housing development, and farming might need to become less aggressively exploitative. We should note that two-thirds of the world's surface does not grow vegetation fit for human consumption, i.e. the sea, the mountains and the polar areas. These areas do yield animals fit for human consumption, though, so it would be unreasonable for all the world to become vegetarian. In areas where both animals and vegetable crops thrive we would need to kill the rabbits, hares, marsupials, birds and other competitors in order to preserve the vegetation for ourselves. Apart from the morality of this, if we are going to kill them, why not eat them? They make very good food.

Diana Sandy, Food and Nutrition Information Service, Cottingham, E. Yorks.

□ EITHER out of necessity or because they follow the tenets of their religion, the great majority of the world's population is already in the non-meat-eating category. It is only the richer third who at present depend on the intensive rearing and slaughter of the animal kingdom – 5 million cows, 14 million pigs, 20 million sheep, 600 million chickens. Contrary to the myths peddled by certain food and nutrition experts, vegetarian food can be as varied, exciting and appetising as anything achieved by *haute cuisine*. Chinese, Mexican, Greek, Indian, Middle Eastern and French culinary skills can transform even the humble tofu or the versatile Quorn and any conceivable vegetable into unforgettable mouth-watering delights. Much more satisfying than the prosaic meat and two veg.

Ifor Rhype, Millend, Glos.

234 *Notes & Queries*

QUESTION: The International Genealogical Index is compiled by the Mormon Church of the Latter Day Saints. Without it, few of us would get far with our family tree. But why have the Mormons gone to such enormous trouble to gather and record all this information from parish records and the like, amounting to millions upon millions of entries from (I believe) many countries?

☐ THIS is to allow them to carry out a process of 'backward baptism'. According to the Mormon Church, when the world ends only Mormons will get to Heaven. Since the Church was only founded in the last century, some of the more perspicacious believers wanted to know why their forebears should have the gates shut in their faces just because the 'truth' had not been available. The Church came up with the idea that if you could trace back your ancestors the whole lot could be baptised posthumously and retrospectively in one job lot with you standing proxy. Although this is an amusing idea to non-believers like myself, it is very offensive to many followers of other faiths, which is why the Mormons have been refused access to some parish registers. All these records are available in this country. Copies are also stored in a nuclear-bomb-proof vault outside Salt Lake City, Nevada, where, when the day comes, hordes of heavenly filing clerks will see who's allowed in.
Clem Turff, Brixton, London SW2.

☐ THE response from Clem Turff contained a number of inaccuracies. Our Church teaches the importance of family relationships, both in this life and the next. Members go to our temples (as distinct from our regular chapels) to have their marriage vows and subsequent parent-to-child ties made not just for this life, but 'for time and all eternity'. We extend those same opportunities to those

of our family who have gone before – as did the early New Testament Christians. The Apostle Paul used this practice as evidence of the reality of resurrection. When speaking to the Corinthian Christians, he said: 'Else what shall they do which are baptised for the dead, if the dead rise not at all? Why are they then baptised for the dead?' (1 Cor. 15:29). That being so, we undertake genealogical research and perform these same ceremonies, by proxy, on behalf of deceased family members. We have no idea, of course, whether they wish to avail themselves of those blessings. Frankly, that's entirely up to them, and we accept their full right to accept or reject the work done on their behalf. We undertake it simply as a labour of love, motivated by an appreciation of those who have gone before. We recognise, of course, that many may not share our theological beliefs, but do have a shared interest in the preservation of those vital records. We are happy to work alongside such people. Currently we are working with the Federation of Family History Societies to transcribe the 1881 Census and make its contents available to all, on microfiche.
Bryan J. Grant, Director of Public Affairs, Church of Jesus Christ of Latter-day Saints, Solihull, W. Midlands.

QUESTION: Why did human beings lose their fur during evolution? It is surely still necessary, and has only resulted in us having to manufacture the replacement or to kill animals?

☐ THE questioner betrays a northern European viewpoint. It is believed that man evolved in equatorial Africa: unusually among mammals, he is adapted to a tropical climate. A constant temperature in the interior of the body obviously depends upon production of heat in the body balancing cooling by the environment. If we take

representative values for the relevant quantities – deep body temperature, heat production, surface area and the insulation provided by the superficial layers of the body – calculation shows that, in an unclothed person at rest, heat production and loss balance at a tropical 28°C. Our bodies have means of adjusting to environments above and below this temperature, but the principal response to cold – increasing heat production by shivering – is not very effective and is subject to fatigue. Sweating, on the other hand, provides man with a means of dissipating excess heat that no other species can match. By contrast, fur-covered animals have insulation that establishes heat balance at much lower temperatures and is widely adjustable (by varying the angle of the hairs, which varies the thickness of the coat); but they have a very limited capacity to increase heat loss. However, using the human body's physiological mechanisms causes discomfort. Humans have developed the technologies of clothing and control of the environment and extended their range away from the tropics. In daily life we constantly adjust clothing and our environment rather than shiver or sweat. We take clothing and shelter largely for granted, but those who enjoy 'outdoor pursuits' can be in a parlous state if they are forced to depend on their innate mechanisms to maintain body temperature.
Professor Romaine Hervey, Wells, Somerset.

INDEX